ONLY GOD KNOWS WHY

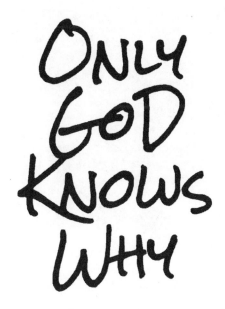

ONLY GOD KNOWS WHY

A Mother's Memoir of Death and Rebirth

AMY LYON

CHALICE
PRESS

ST. LOUIS, MISSOURI

Cover image: karenroach/Bigstock.com
Cover design: Elizabeth Wright

www.chalicepress.com

8 7 6 5 4 3 2 1   12 13 14 15 16 17 18

Library of Congress Cataloging-in-Publication Data

Lyon, Amy, 1976-
Only God knows why : a mother's memoir of death and rebirth / Amy Lyon.
   p. cm.
Includes bibliographical references and index.
ISBN 978-0-8272-2752-1 (alk. paper) ISBN 978-0-8272-2753-8 (EPUB)
ISBN 978-0-8272-2754-5 (EPDF)
   1. Children—Death—Religious aspects—Christianity. 2. Bereavement—Religious aspects—Christianity. 3. Grief—Religious aspect—Christianity. 4. Mothers—Religious life. 5. Consolation. 6. Lyon, Amy, 1976- I. Title.

BV4907.L96 2012
248.8'66092—dc23
[B]   2012028179

Printed in the United States of America

Dedication
For my children, who have inspired me beyond belief.
And for my husband, who is indeed the man of my dreams.

Contents

Chapter One

I was in my condo washing the yellow Pyrex mixing bowl I'd swiped from Mom's house when I first thought it:

It might be fun to have a family of my own someday.

From there my thoughts turned to having a baby and I was annoyed, at first, by the notion of excess baggage weighing down my light load. "No kids" had been my mantra since seventh-grade health class and it hadn't occurred to me until then to change my tune. As I grew into my early twenties, several of my friends shared dreams of large families, but I never thought that far ahead. Whoever coined the phrase, "Live in the moment," had me in mind.

But that day, washing dishes, my mind ran wild like I was a five-year-old playing house. I imagined my husband and my child—a faceless, nameless little sprout—urging me to finish the dishes so we could head off to the Hennepin County Fair.

"Just a minute," I would tell my little family with a syrupy sweet voice that could put June Cleaver to shame. "I can't bear the thought of coming home to dirty dishes."

My imaginary child would tug on my leg and plead, "Pleeeease, Mommy," and I would wipe my hands on the dish towel and throw it on the counter.

"Oh, what the heck!" I'd say. "The dishes can wait!"

My mind perked up at the family fantasy, despite the fact that there was nothing *Leave it to Beaver* about my current lifestyle. I was freshly single, had recently bought my own two-bedroom condo, worked full-time as the editor of a weekly community newspaper, and went out more nights than I stayed in. I was twenty-four and incredibly proud of the work I did, especially since my college education ended with a two-year associate of arts degree from a local community college. I had started as an intern at the weekly newspaper a few months after turning twenty, and over the next four years I'd worked my way up the small company's ladder from intern to receptionist to staff reporter to assistant editor and finally, to editor.

Dad had a tendency to announce my title to random acquaintances when we were together. I was the first one in our family to go to college, unless of course you counted Dad's auto body classes at Dunwoody Technical Institute. He couldn't spell to save his life and Mom said some of her worst childhood memories involved writing papers for school. So, it was a mystery to our entire family how I'd picked up the writing gene.

The chaos of the newspaper world had a way of bringing out the best and the worst in me. Looming deadlines molded me into what the position required: a strong-minded, "work-is-my-life" twenty-something that was content with an income hovering just above poverty level.

I had recently vowed to take a break from serious relationships. The one-, two-, and three-year relationships that had followed each other back to back left me concerned that the next one might be four years and I'd wind up just as empty-hearted. I maintained an active social life with my coworkers, though, mixing business and pleasure like a high-octane cocktail.

Janelle sold advertising and was single, too. She called me "Little Lulu" and quickly became the big sister I'd never had. She was genuine and supportive of all of my decisions, especially when I announced to her that I needed to fill my free time with yoga and kickboxing classes. She gently pointed out that I was too high strung to relax into a yoga class and there wasn't an aggressive bone in my body for kickboxing. I knew she was right, but I needed to fill my time. It was hard for me to be alone—used to the company of *someone,* even if he wasn't *the one*—and I reasoned that the yoga and kickboxing classes could propel me into a new dimension where I could learn how to feel comfortable by myself. And, just as important, the classes would undoubtedly tone my body, which would be a bonus when Mr. Right did come along.

"But you do what you need to do, Little Lulu," she said to me on the phone the afternoon of my twenty-fourth birthday. "It's all about taking care of you now."

That night I celebrated at her apartment in Minneapolis. She'd invited several of our friends from work and some friends I'd never met. She baked me a chocolate cake with a flaming "24" candle on top.

"This is going to be the best year yet," she whispered to me as someone took our picture...

The next day was a Sunday and I woke crumpled in a hung-over ball on Janelle's futon, which she lovingly covered with blue and yellow daisy sheets on the nights she figured I'd be staying over. As I lay there, face down, I tried to piece together the events from the night before. Each time I thought I had compiled a complete rundown of goings-on for the night, another scene played out on the backs of my eyelids, and the more that came, the more mortified I felt.

I pushed myself up slowly and sat on the edge of the futon, then collected the contents of my purse, which were strewn next to me. I flipped open my cell phone and saw an unfamiliar number, then noticed that I had had a conversation with the owner of that unfamiliar number for nearly an hour after bar close. I wanted to wake Janelle to ask her about the mystery person but, like me, she wasn't much of a morning person. I flipped the phone shut and saw that it wasn't even 8 a.m. I felt sick to my stomach, but even more disconcerting was the unexplainable urge I had to go to church. I wanted to confess my sins and do whatever it was that good Christians did to make themselves feel clean in their own dirty skins. However, I only knew for sure of one Lutheran church in the metro area besides my childhood institution, which I had vowed never to step foot inside again. The stench of being reprimanded in confirmation class for questioning the validity of Mary's Immaculate Conception still hung too fresh in the air. And I was pretty sure it was against the rules to go to a church outside of the denomination in which you were raised.

Propelled by who knows what, I straightened my tank top with a quick yank, unfurled my jeans from their tight twist around my legs, collected my belongings and slipped into my shoes—still sticky from spilled drinks the night before. I headed toward home, a two-bedroom condo just outside of Minneapolis that I'd bought that spring. It was located in the city where my parents grew up and near the high school from which they both graduated. Although my mom, dad and younger sister had moved to Florida a few months earlier after my dad's retirement, I took comfort in walking the streets Mom and Dad had walked as teenagers and eating at some of the restaurants they'd visited while dating. It connected us despite the distance. Now my parents were in the process of a fairly-civilized divorce and, ironically, I felt close to them as I pulled into the parking lot of Gethsemane Lutheran Church where they were married thirty-two years earlier.

Happy families made their way into the bright white, square-shaped church. There was a traditional Mary-and-the-halo stained-glass window out front and off to the side an enormous white steeple jutted toward the sky as if to scream, *I'm overcompensating for something!*

I parked and popped open the glove box. No mints. I raked a brush through my tangled hair, which I'd recently dyed from blonde to "crushed garnet."

"What am I doing here?" I grumbled as I slid out of the car and headed toward the entrance. Halfway there, I dared to look down at my ensemble. In a sea of fresh faces and crisply dressed children of God, I stood out like a ragamuffin—maybe still a little drunk from the night before. Grandpa once told me that God didn't care how you came to church as long as you got yourself there, and I sure hoped that was true.

The double doors had colorful panes of stained glass and an elderly gentleman pulled the wooden entrance open for me. "Welcome," he said, and I felt like we were off to a good start, this church and me. But then the stares came as I walked into the waiting area on the way to the sanctuary and I knew Grandpa was wrong. These people *did* care how I came to *their* church. I could read the judgment in their expressions as they sipped coffee from mugs that should have been inscribed with the words: *Regular member who tithes.* I felt so far away from my comfort zone that I couldn't even turn around and run. So, I pretended to be one of those aloof girls who march to the beat of their own drums and just didn't care what other people thought about the tune. For all they knew, I'd carefully selected that particular pair of jeans, top, and flip-flops out of my closet that very morning, rather than the morning before.

I slid into a spot at the end of a pew near the back of the church. During the opening prayer I linked my fingers together and spotted faded markings on my palm. I looked more closely and made out numbers scribbled onto my skin, the same number I had called after bar close. I tried to smear the digits away with my thumb, but the ink was there to stay.

It was very possible I dozed off during the sermon. The whole deal seemed to wrap up pretty quickly, and when everyone shuffled up for communion, I stayed put. I felt like a little demon was using my intestines as a slip-and-slide and I didn't want to risk the "body and blood" triggering my gag reflex. I thought about ducking out when my row headed up front, but I was determined to push through and get something out of this service. Some sort of quick fix. After all, that was what I was there for, wasn't it? My life just didn't feel right, so I came to God, to his house of worship. The least he could do was inspire me.

When we stood for the last gospel reading, hot flashes pulsated behind my eyeballs, and the little brat next to me obnoxiously squeezed herself between her mother and the pew in front of them.

"Mommy, no!" she hissed as her mother forced her back into the space next to me. "She smells like stinky cigarettes."

My face burned and I tried to step to my left but hit the edge of the pew. I was trapped, again, in a church, just like the days of confirmation class. I stared straight ahead, my heart pounding as I recited the Lord's Prayer from memory. That little ditty had been burned into my brain.

As soon as the pastor began the closing prayer and the other church-goers shuffled their belongings together, I snatched my purse off the floor and high-tailed it out the side door. I knew better. I was not a church person and never would become one. All of those little androids reciting words written by other people annoyed me... Half of them looked comatose and no one looked happy. Weren't people supposed to be happy at church? Or maybe they just saw church services as mandatory meetings to qualify them for entrance into Heaven. Either way, it wasn't my scene.

I shoved into my car and glanced in the rearview mirror. My heart lurched up into my throat. The random digits written on my hand from the night before had transferred themselves onto my left cheek sometime during the night. Just like little scarlet letters.

* * *

It was during this time in my life that I met Mr. Chad Lyon through a friend of mine at the newspaper. Chad came out to the bars with us on a few occasions—when he didn't have Army reservist training the next day—and I always thought he seemed fun. *A fun friend.* He had a girlfriend he'd met while he was at a language school in Monterey, and they lived together in an apartment only a few blocks from my condo. We joked that we could meet in the middle and take a walk some day.

One night, Chad shared with the group the details of the rocky relationship with his girlfriend and how they had recently "broken up." I knew that story too well. Each of my relationships had been a continuous cycle of on-again, off-again, and I had enough sense not to get involved with someone who was in that kind of relationship. The timing was off for Chad and me anyway and that was okay. After the church incident, I took my single status seriously. I wanted to learn how to be alone and how to identify what I wanted in a partner, maybe even a husband. I had a tendency to latch on to anyone just to have someone and I often lost myself in the process. Still, sometimes Chad and I held hands at the bar while having long conversations about nothing important.

Then, in the fall, Chad moved out of the apartment he shared with his girlfriend and announced that they were officially done. He took his cat to his dad's house on the other side of town, and our weekly phone conversations increased. We went to a haunted house and hayride for Halloween, and I followed close to Chad as he led me through the maze of black lights and strobe effects. I used the haunted house as an excuse to walk close to him and, finally, to reach for his hand. On the hayride, he sat next to me and put his arm around my shoulders. He was strong and steadfast and I felt safe by his side.

I was reluctant to relax, though, because I had developed an image in my mind of my next boyfriend, the potential husband of my imaginary child, and my only criteria were that he have a good job, have muscles, and measure at least six-feet tall. Chad had a strong build, "a wrestler's body," my gay friend had said, and I was definitely attracted to his enormous brown eyes and dark hair—sort of a young George Clooney. He managed a GNC, and I felt that that was a good job for a twenty-six-year-old. The only problem was that Chad was the same height as me: five-foot-seven. I wanted to stick to my guns on the height issue, and although I had fun when we hung out, he didn't match my profile.

"So, what's the deal with us?" Chad asked on a Saturday night before Christmas as we snuggled on my couch watching a movie.

I shrugged. "What do you mean?"

Chad didn't pursue the matter, and the more I tried to keep our status casual, the more my feelings for him swelled around my heart, urging me to let him in. And the more time I spent with him, the less important the height issue became. (In fact, more than a decade later, I would cringe at the realization that I was so superficial and, more importantly, that I could have screwed things up, maybe even lost him, over something so silly.)

The final nudge came the day before Christmas. It was a children's book Chad had ordered for his two-year-old nephew, Nick. It was personalized to make Nick a key character in the story. Chad brought the book to my house before we went out to dinner. He wanted me to see the purchase he was so proud of before it was wrapped. As he slowly turned each page, reading out loud, he beamed and I was nudged. I fell over the edge, head first in love with Chad Lyon.

After that, things moved quickly for us. A few days after Christmas I met his family and joined them for a holiday weekend getaway in Spicer, Wisconsin. We snowmobiled, sledded, and celebrated the holiday in a little local bar. A month after that we flew to Florida where I introduced Chad to my family, and when we returned from our trip, he moved into my condo. I reasoned that we might as well cohabitate since his cat, Guinness, had stayed at my place during our trip and had gotten to know my cat, Pixie.

"It would be a shame to separate them," I said.

Nine months after that, Chad and I gave notice at our jobs and moved to Florida to be closer to my family. We dreamed of a convertible car, no snow, learning to surf and making new friends. What we hadn't bargained for was our homesickness, inability to find work, or that the day-to-day life in Florida was nothing like the vacation we'd hoped for. We lived with my mom and sister for a few months, then bought a three-bedroom foreclosure home for $56,000. We were determined to make it work, and we made a good team as we powered through to fix up the 1,100-square-foot house in an effort to make it our home. We roofed together, tiled together, painted together, and landscaped together. We learned quickly that most things were better when we did them together.

Six months after that, while home in Minnesota for the holidays, Chad asked me to marry him. He was raised Catholic and that presented some challenges for me. I fretted for several days over how to tell Chad, simply, that I wasn't a fan...of any of it: *Religion. The church. The men in robes.* And when I finally did tell him that I didn't want to get married in an unfamiliar church (or any church, really) he agreed that it would be all right to go with my plan of being married on the beach by a stranger who happened to have a license to wed. I'd plucked her name out of the newspaper and met briefly with Laura in the kitchen of her lower-level condo in a nearby city called Satellite Beach.

"I talk a little bit about God, you know, traditional things, but mostly focus on the couple," she said. "The typical ceremony is short and sweet, and, most important, it's legal."

I laughed when she laughed, and then I confided in her that I'd adopted a new stance on religion, something I'd overheard a lady say while waiting in line at Wal-Mart: *I'm not for organized religion. I have my own relationship with the man upstairs.*

Chad didn't question my reasoning. He picked his battles with me, I knew, and usually agreed to most anything I wanted if it didn't hurt anyone or make him look stupid.

Our ceremony overlooking the beach and the reception in the beach-front hotel turned out perfectly. We were lucky enough to have eighty-eight friends and family members fly from Minnesota to the east coast of Florida for the event. It rained all day—with a half-hour break in the weather that conveniently occurred at the time of our nuptials. We even had time for a few photos before the sky opened up again and everyone hurried inside.

My sister, Kim, was my maid of honor and I had four bridesmaids: Janelle, two friends from high school Jen and Marti, and a former coworker named Yvonne. The next day was also rainy and Jen suggested we visit a tattoo parlor. She was the last person in the world who would normally suggest something so radical, so I went along with her, thinking it couldn't be all bad. We got matching daisy tattoos on our lower backs, called ourselves the "Daisy Girls," and vowed to remain close, despite our distance.

Most likely it was seeing everyone again that helped Chad and me make the decision to move back to Minnesota that fall. It was two years to the date when we loaded up another big, yellow moving truck and hauled ourselves north. Looking back, there was good and there was bad that came from our stint in Florida. Chad had transferred down to the Sunshine State with GNC, lost his job on my birthday and started in a management position with Walgreens. The company granted his request to transfer from Florida to Minnesota, and he wound up working in the same town where my parents had lived and where I'd owned my condo two years earlier.

Unfortunately, in my absence, Janelle had moved to Texas, a strange dream she'd always had even though she had no connections to the place. She was a woman on the move, though, and always made friends quickly. I, however, was not so lucky with friends or with work in Florida. I had attempted to find a full-time job at a newspaper, but only landed a freelance gig for a weekly publication that helped pay the bills, but didn't quite cover them. So, I took a job slinging cocktails on a casino ship out of Port Canaveral and experienced a breakdown of sorts when I realized my career trajectory was going backward, not forward.

I loved being close to my family, but Chad and I agreed we would never raise children in Florida. And while it felt strange to talk about children with Chad because of my "no kids" policy, being with my new husband made me think differently about a lot of things.

Chapter Two

When I turned thirty, married for only three years, I wanted desperately to find someone or something to save me from myself. I felt the uneasiness of it in my bones, and while I didn't know who could save me and how exactly they'd do it, I was constantly searching. I didn't share my anxiety with anyone. I knew I'd get little or no sympathy. I was married to Chad, a terrific man with a secure job that gave us health insurance and money for a far-away retirement. We owned a cozy three-bedroom home in Minnesota on almost an acre of land. We had all of the luxuries a middle-class couple needed and most of what we wanted. But I wanted more and it wasn't necessarily material things. I wondered daily if "this was it," if this was really all there was to my life. I made lists of what was good and bad in my life, and the good always outweighed the bad. Always. In fact, often times I had to force myself to find petty annoyances to write in the bad column: *sometimes my neighbor plays his CDs (Cher's* Heart of Stone *album) late at night and I can't sleep* or *My cell phone doesn't get very good reception inside the house and I have to go outside to take calls.*

The more I mulled it over, the less I knew what I wanted. But something clearly was missing from my life. I hadn't written anything in years aside from a few freelance articles, and I stopped journaling all together. I obtained my real estate license when we moved back to Minnesota in order to make more money and I worried about money constantly. I had a thirty-five minute commute to the real estate office and I spent most of that time anticipating the worst. During the rest of the drive I wondered if I was just one of those annoying people who could never be satisfied. There were people starving and dying all over the world, but *I just didn't feel right.*

As I balanced my checkbook one evening, I highlighted all of the areas where I could cut back. The number of restaurants and bars I frequented overwhelmed me, so I launched into a tirade.

"Chad! You need to start bringing your lunch to work!" I spat as he cooked dinner. "We need to pay off all of these bills."

He didn't say anything and that fueled my fire even more. He wasn't the real problem. I knew that in my heart. The problem was that I wasn't married to my husband, and I wasn't married to my job; I was married to my coworkers and the various bars in the western suburb of Minneapolis that we frequented. And even though I was aware of that sad fact, it did nothing to change my behavior.

The town where I grew up was, by that time, an upscale area around a beautiful lake west of the Twin Cities. During my childhood, the area was mostly cabins and modest-sized homes—nothing like the McMansion Central it had since become. Chad sometimes joked—at least I thought he was joking—and called me an elitist when I wore my "Locals Only" sweatshirt that promoted the area. And when I chose to sell real estate there rather than the sweet southern suburb we lived in, it was that elitist mentality I tried to hone. It didn't matter that hobnobbing wasn't my forte. I wanted money. Lots and lots of money. I was prepared to do what I needed to do to obtain my riches even if it meant morphing into someone else to please a client. I was convinced that money would solve my identity crisis.

I was a successful real estate agent and I learned to love important things, such as high-heeled shoes in various colors, Kate Spade purses, and jet black eyeliner. I loved happy hour because I was good at it and I knew my role. I was that person who everyone wanted to know was coming. I made the evening fun and I encouraged explosive and uncomfortable conversations that ultimately drove everyone to drink more. Drinking wasn't a problem for me, at least I didn't see it as a problem. I never craved booze and I didn't feel like I needed a drink in the middle of the day to keep me going. I was a social drinker and it was that social scene that kept reeling me in.

One night several of us hit the local watering hole for an early happy hour and I was tipsy within an hour—celebrating the earnings of a closing that afternoon. We wound up at another bar that I don't recall visiting, but I do remember that I called my husband from a coworker's house at nearly midnight. The coworker's family was out of town, so I can only imagine the rage Chad felt when he came to the guy's house, peeled me off the bathroom floor and carried me out to his truck. I fell asleep on his lap on the drive home and woke up once to him hitting the steering wheel and cussing. That night as we lay in bed he asked me if I was having an affair.

"God no!" I blurted and cuddled up next to him with my eyelids pressed tight to minimize the room's spinning. "I just don't know how to do this. I don't know how to be a good wife."

Chad wasn't a big talker and, again, he didn't comment. As I drifted in and out of consciousness, I thought about telling him I *was* actually having an affair. I looked to happy hour and my coworkers for emotional fulfillment.

The stories the next day at the office were horrendous, and one story spread like front-page news: I had found the white pool-table chalk at the bar and made a game out of slapping my hand prints on my own rear end. Apparently one of the other girls followed suit and we spent the night wagging our backsides to anyone who would look. I'm sure it seemed sexy in the midst of intoxication, but sober, I was mortified.

In my healthier days I had written a column for a New Age magazine referring to my body as a temple (no religious reference intended) and how my building had solid bones and a strong foundation due to the effort I put into its maintenance. On this particular day, I thought that if my body ever was the temple I touted it to be, it was nearing the point of condemnation. The bulldozers were coming and, strangely, I seemed to be the one guiding them.

After the butt-print incident, I had an intense urge to be different. I went home every night and resisted the invitations to happy hour. I couldn't handle the back and forth between two contradicting lifestyles—one of the elitist real estate agent making oodles of money to attain her one goal in life of financial freedom, and one of a happily-married wife in the suburbs who worked during the day, loved to write, and enjoyed evenings with her family and friends. But the latter seemed too laid back, too "mom-like." I worried life would pass me by if I gave up my freedom so soon.

I operated in a constant state of restlessness and quickly succumbed to panic attacks. I called Chad in a tizzy on more than one occasion, convinced I was having a heart attack or suffocating. Obviously I wasn't the type of person to look to God for help, but I did pray once that he would save me from my impending death during the claustrophobic effects of downtown traffic. Of course, I emerged from the traffic unscathed, but considering my history with God, or lack thereof, who could blame me for not seeking his help more often? I did wonder why this almighty, powerful being didn't guide me like he reportedly guided other people. I'd had plenty of crap dropped in my lap in thirty years and never once did he run toward me with a shovel. And that was why I was determined not to rely on any sort of higher power. I did fine on my own and held fast to the idea that praying was for people with real problems, such as cancer, or for soldiers fighting overseas. And as far as asking for forgiveness went, well, there were people such as rapists and pedophiles who really needed to move to the front of that line. My sins were small potatoes.

Still, part of me screamed out that my life wasn't right. I heard a constant buzzing in my ears, like the background static of a radio that's tuned into a station, but the reception is just a little off. It was the loudest, sourceless sound I'd ever heard and it plagued me day and night. I went to the doctor complaining of tinnitus symptoms, and he instructed me to flush my ears daily with warm water and to sleep more.

I found a Web site where other people experiencing panic attacks gathered and I posted a few thoughts in the comments section about what I was experiencing. Just my luck, the first response came from a woman in Mississippi who told me to pray about the situation and let God show me the way. I logged off the site and never went back. I steered clear of anyone who might lead me to a conversation with God. I was completely turned off by strict Christians who claimed a person had to pray the rosary on some set schedule, tithe ten percent of earnings to the church, or complete a dozen other rituals for entrance into Heaven.

I rationalized that real estate had to be the right career for me, even though I dreaded showing properties and really didn't care if people got the house they wanted as long as I didn't have to shuttle them around in my car every weekend. The job had to be right for me because I made good money. Wasn't that the telltale sign of success? Or maybe Maya Angelou had it all figured out when she said, "Making a living is not the same as making a life."

I endured several months of daily panic attacks before I sat myself down and demanded, out loud, that I change something about my life. I looked online and found a local anxiety support group that met once a month. In the basement of a community center, a middle-aged man talked about how he couldn't get out of bed some mornings and often clutched his teddy bear like it was his source of oxygen. Another woman said she became immobilized over the weekend while shopping in a department store with her mother.

"I had a 10 on the 1–10 scale of panic attacks," she said.

I knew what a "10" panic attack felt like. I continued to listen as the group of a dozen or so shared ways to deal with anxiety on a day-to-day basis. Everything from relaxation breathing to calming herbs to exercise was discussed. I realized quickly that these weren't the conversations I wanted to have. I wanted to know why my anxiety was here and I wanted to know how I could get rid of it for good. I didn't care about all of the stuff in between and, frankly, I didn't have time for it.

I knew Chad wanted a baby, and the topic of a little one came up several times that spring. Each time we talked about becoming parents, the idea of having a baby seemed more appealing to me. I imagined a child with my energy and Chad's patience. I imagined myself feeling fulfilled. I imagined the little person saving me from myself. More than any of that, I wanted to have a baby with Chad for the right reasons. I recalled several talk shows I'd seen over the years that reminded dysfunctional people that having a baby couldn't fix all that was wrong in one's life, but instead usually complicated the situation further. I didn't want to be that mother and I didn't want to bring a baby into an unhealthy situation. So I made a list of what I liked and what I didn't like about my life, *again,* and wrote down what I felt I needed to change. I was entirely honest with myself and it became apparent when I took away the buddies and the booze that selling real estate gave me no creative outlet.

As spring rolled into summer, I found myself dreading phone calls from new clients even though that was supposed to be the most exciting part of the sales job. The thrill of the chase and…*BAM!* Got a client! My bread and butter. I felt no satisfaction at the closing table other than a gleeful tick that I could put another check in the bank to pay our mortgage. I couldn't admit to anyone, not even to Chad, that I wasn't satisfied selling real estate. Especially not after I'd spent the time and money to get my real estate license while my friends and family supported me emotionally and Chad supported us financially.

I'd started taking a low dose anti-depressant to help with my anxiety and decided to go off the pills while Chad and I attempted to get pregnant. We got pregnant on the first try and when I shared the exciting news with my coworkers—my supposed buddies—they quickly distanced themselves from me as if I'd told them I had the bird flu rather than morning sickness. That's when it finally registered: they really were just bar buddies, and, knowing that I wouldn't touch a drop of alcohol during pregnancy, they didn't need me anymore.

So, I spent my first trimester working from home while attempting to keep a leash on my runaway hormones. I got a day-by-day guide detailing the goings-on inside my body, and I shared the daily progress with Chad when he arrived home each night. We marveled at all of the amazing pieces that needed to fall into place to make one tiny human being.

"Did you know the baby already displays a reflex response to touch?" I asked Chad one evening, reading over the day's developments. "At 44 days! And by today, 'the indentations at your baby's knees and ankles are present.' It hasn't even been in there two months!"

Chad laughed and told me I was cute, then he rubbed my belly. I felt good about our decision. I walked nearly every day, winding around the tree-lined streets of our neighborhood. Our black lab mix, Raven, stopped yanking me through the neighbors' yards when she saw squirrels or bunnies, and I guessed she knew there was something special happening inside my body. In my spare time, which I allowed myself quite a bit of, I talked to my ever-expanding waistline and promised the little person growing inside of me that I would lead the healthiest lifestyle possible.

Throughout the winter, I continued to exercise at the local gym and walked on the treadmill three times a week. I felt proud of the baby bump that stretched the fabric of Chad's T-shirts, and I noticed gym-goers' eyes on me, on my belly, as I edged near three miles per hour on the treadmill. The mild activity of walking became exhausting for me at 36 weeks, and I cut out the cardio and resorted to stretching exercises at home for the last leg of my pregnancy.

I sold a few houses during that eight months, but I didn't exert any extra effort to find clients. I had a mad case of nesting mania and only wanted to think about the baby girl growing and kicking inside my tummy—a girl Chad and I decided to name Isabelle Leeann Lyon. Isabelle because Chad suggested the name and I liked it, and Leeann because Lee was my mom's and my middle name and Ann was my sister's middle name.

And as it goes in the real estate world, the weekend I was due to deliver Isabelle, a couple I knew from the newspaper decided it was time to find their dream house. I felt ridiculously euphoric and pain free, yet Chad didn't trust me out alone. He had already lined our king-size mattress with a sheet of plastic traditionally used in home remodeling, and outfitted the driver's seat of my car with a black plastic bag and beach towel. He was convinced my water would break in one of those two places. Chad was my chauffeur that weekend as we showed my clients six houses just outside of Minneapolis, one of which they chose to make their home. We wrote up an offer on my due date, and Chad and I went into the local real estate office and faxed the offer to the seller's agent the morning I was in labor. One of my coworkers, Pete, offered to handle the transaction while I was in the hospital. Pete was one of the agents from my office who'd contacted me on a regular basis to see how I was doing, and he genuinely seemed to care.

My labor stretched over 36 hours. I had an epidural about halfway through, and Chad and I spent most of the time in the hospital watching HGTV. I had a bad case of the shakes at about 30 hours and was convinced I was having the mother of all anxiety attacks. My pulse skyrocketed and stayed up until the nurse on duty informed me that the medications and hormone fluctuations often made women twitchy during labor. To help me relax, the nurses let me catch the newest episodes of "Design on a Dime" and "House Hunters" in between pushes.

Isabelle was a big girl: 8 pounds, 3 ounces; 21 inches long with tons of dark hair. Visitors immediately noticed that she looked like her dad and I felt pride swell inside of me. The first evening in the hospital, while I watched Chad hold our little girl and practice the swaddling technique he'd learned from one of the nurses, I thought that my life finally felt perfect. The search was over. Finally, I had a purpose. I would take care of this baby girl and I would be an incredible mother.

Cute little outfits were lined up in her closet in graduated sizes. Onesies—short-sleeve and long—were stacked in her dresser, and a brand new Diaper Genie was in place. At the first twinges of contractions, I'd unboxed the A&D Ointment, the blue nose sucker, and the baby thermometer. I was ahead of the game.

So it was, on the day she was born, I was gloriously blissful, ignorant of the dark path rising up to meet me. And nothing and no one could have prepared me for what I'd soon be up against.

Chapter Three

I was overwhelmed, and not in a good way, by all of the visitors who came to see us in the hospital. But how could I tell proud grandparents and excited aunts and uncles to go home? The groups that filtered in nonstop didn't even include my mom and sister, who were due to arrive from Florida three days later. I tried to relax and tried to be perky for the guests like a new mom should be, knowing that Chad just wanted to show off his baby. But I felt irritated with every, "Knock knock! Where's the little girl?" or, "I heard someone had a baby in here!"

By the third day, I burst into tears whenever Chad announced that someone was coming to the hospital to see Isabelle. We were discharged that afternoon, and when we got home, it was as if I stood in someone else's kitchen, in someone else's life, unsure of what to do next. That evening I locked myself in the bathroom and soaked in the bathtub until my skin puckered just so I wouldn't have to play hostess to another batch of visitors. I couldn't catch my breath and I thought that if I did catch it, I wouldn't know what to do with it. Just like I didn't know what to do with Isabelle. She was so perfect and so little, and I felt like everything I'd learned in my life up to that point was useless. Nothing could have prepared me for her. For my feelings about her.

I couldn't even change her diaper right. Chad gave Isabelle her first bath in a tiny tub that fit inside our kitchen sink, and he was the one who dressed and undressed her. She seemed like a fragile piece of china that belonged to someone else, and I felt awful thinking it, but I wanted to set her aside on a shelf until I felt grown up enough to touch her.

I did know how to breastfeed her, though. I was naturally good at that, so those were the precious moments we spent together. But even then I couldn't wrap my brain around the fact that she was mine... *forever and ever*, and I found myself annoyed with the way she drifted off to sleep halfway through her feeding and then awoke hungry an hour later. I wondered how someone so small could exhaust me so completely.

At her first appointment three days later, the doctor said she was a perfectly healthy baby aside from a slight case of jaundice, a fairly common occurrence in newborns. There was just one other problem, though, our pediatrician told us.

"Her test results came back positive for cystic fibrosis," Dr. Philip said, and gave me the instructions for a sweat test Isabelle would need to have at Children's Hospital in Minneapolis.

I examined Isabelle's face and wondered what a baby with cystic fibrosis looked like. Was it anything like Down's syndrome, in which you could often see the signs in the baby's lips, in the set of the eyes, or in certain mannerisms? I looked up the disease on WebMD and found that it mainly affected the lungs and digestive system, and got progressively worse. It was also hereditary and I didn't know of anyone in my family or Chad's with cystic fibrosis. More than that, I was horrified that there was even a possibility that we could have a baby with a problem, let alone a disease. That kind of thing didn't happen to *us*. It happened to other people in remote towns I'd never heard of, and I cursed God before I even got the test results. Once again he'd let me down.

Two days later the test results came back negative and all of my worrying was for nothing. I breathed a sigh of relief and felt thankful that my perfect baby girl was still perfectly healthy. God didn't get a second thought and certainly didn't receive an apology for my tantrums sent in his direction. He shouldn't have put me through the worrying, I thought. And despite the good news, there was something there, lurking at the back of my mind with all of that brain matter researchers say never gets used. A shadow, a being of some sort nagging at me, making my head and my body pulsate with unease. How was it that, in the happiest time of my life, I felt anything but happy?

"What the hell is wrong with me?" I spat one evening when Isabelle and I were alone, and I wondered why I wanted to be anywhere in the world except holding my new baby. That certainly wasn't normal.

And despite the fact that Isabelle's sweet little personality developed a little bit more each day, the days alone with her seemed harder and harder for me once my mom and sister went back to Florida and Chad went back to work. She was not a difficult baby by any means, and according to the horror stories I'd heard about infants with colic and acid reflux, she was one of the lowest maintenance babies ever made. She was easily soothed and able to self soothe already at three weeks.

I had started freelance writing again during my last two months of pregnancy and had decided not to take a maternity leave from assignments. I didn't think I needed a break. Instead I kept working from home, where I wrote for the newspaper and edited a lifestyle magazine. I'd also started an online craft business called Daisy Glass for glass bottle art I created in a kiln, and that generated two to three orders per week through a Web site. I'd thought a break from real estate was what I needed when I took on the writing gigs, but later I realized that it was a break from everything that could have saved my sanity in those first weeks after Isabelle was born.

It didn't help that I had idyllic fantasies of being one of *those* moms who could juggle the job, the housekeeping, the bills, and every last detail without putting her child in day care—even though I knew working on my articles in the evenings wasn't an option because Chad was finishing up his business management degree online. So, I tried to work during the day while I was alone with Isabelle. I made lists with check boxes in front of the to-do items and put so many demands on myself that I nearly burst one night from the weight of my world. I blamed Isabelle for my inability to do *anything* because all she wanted was to be held and fed. I didn't know how to be a mom and it seemed I wasn't very good at it instinctually.

Chad was accustomed to my ongoing quest to be the next Superwoman. In our six years together, I'd never been one to sit still for a moment or relax, thanks to the high-strung gene from my dad's side of the family, but even Chad recommended one night that I take it easy and let my body heal. I didn't listen. I couldn't. There was a voice in my head pushing me and pushing me to try harder, to do more, to do it all, and to do it now.

Most days I felt like a failure. All of the boxes on my to-do list weren't checked off and I refused to ask for help. Each time Chad's family members offered assistance, cleaning help, or babysitting, I denied their requests. Acceptance was a sign of weakness and I didn't want to feel like I owed anybody anything. Chad's sister, Andre, took Isabelle to her house a few miles away on several occasions, and rather than relax for the evening like Chad suggested, I edited stories or did laundry or melted glass bottles. Soon, in any given day, I cried more than Isabelle. I couldn't keep up and I felt guilty that I often thought of Isabelle as a burden preventing me from accomplishing my many tasks, preventing me from living my normal life.

I had a hard time sleeping at night. Chad's other sister, Jennie, came over during the days so I could nap, but I still couldn't sleep. I passed time by staring at the ceiling, anticipating some unidentifiable horror that was headed my way. My once-favorite pastime of afternoon naps became a dreaded task that I worried about and literally lost sleep over. They were great plans I had to be Superwoman, but it seemed that in my planning I had forgotten to factor Isabelle into the mix.

By week four, I fully resented the sweet little baby who only desired my love. Being a new mom wasn't at all what I had expected it to be, or even a smidgen of what *Parents* magazine promised. I figured it was my fault I sucked at being a mom. I felt guilty and awful and fat and lost. I longed for my old life. Maybe it wasn't perfect, but at least it was familiar. I resented Chad for his escape to work for full days.

"Work? You're jealous because I get to go to work?" he asked me one morning as he flipped his tie into a perfect knot. "I'd rather be home with Isabelle!"

"See, that's the problem!" I cried. "Why don't I want to be home with Isabelle?"

"You're just tired," he rationalized and pointed to her crib. "She's sleeping now. You should be sleeping."

I huffed and lay back down. *Sleep when your baby sleeps.* Whoever coined that phrase must have been a man. A very stupid man who worked for *Parents* magazine.

As day rolled into night rolled into day, I became more convinced that I couldn't do it, the whole mom thing. I slept in Isabelle's room on a futon. It was easier to get up with her in the middle of the night and we kept, to date, my favorite apparatus in the room: a small cooler and bottle warmer. Isabelle fussed so badly one night that I didn't get one minute of sleep. Jennie came over the next day for my regularly scheduled nap, but when I lay down, my mind buzzed. And that night, even though Isabelle slept, I lay wide awake, the music of some distant merry-go-round playing in my head.

By morning I was sobbing so uncontrollably that I couldn't even tell Chad what was wrong with me when he came into the nursery to check on us.

"I'm fine," I said through hyperventilating gasps and waved him off. "I'm just tired."

He took my word for it and went to work. I tried to lay Isabelle in bed with me, but she was hungry and she was ready to get up. She'd had a good night's sleep. She gave a squeal of protest when I tried to lay her next to me and irritation raced through my veins and made my temper flare. I buried my face in a pillow, then hit the pillow repeatedly like a mad woman. I must have scared her, and when she started to howl, I turned quickly and shouted, "I hate you!" then left the room. I cried on the bathroom floor for several minutes, then, fearing she might roll off the bed, I hurried back into the nursery where she continued to cry.

"I don't hate you," I whispered and pulled her to my chest. "Mommy just doesn't know what to do. I don't know how to take care of you or what to do!"

My words apparently flipped her happy-baby switch, because she stopped crying and snuggled into my neck. And though the closeness felt good after my outburst, I was freshly blanketed in guilt. All she wanted was her mommy. What the hell was wrong with me? I was her source of comfort and I didn't believe I'd earned that right. Why did she even want me? I was a wreck and losing, by the minute, the pieces that held me together.

While I changed her diaper I tried to smile because I had read in *Parents* magazine that babies are extremely in tune to their moms' emotions and affected by facial expressions. The magazine instructed me to smile, so I did. But I was convinced this little girl saw right through to the core of me and knew how awful I felt. I didn't want her to think my breakdown was her fault. Whatever was going on with me had very little to do with her; I knew that, but did she? I continued to smile as tears wetted my cheeks, and I played with her little toes to assure her that, somewhere, I had it in me to be a good mom. Good moms played with their babies' toes.

We went downstairs and I made her a bottle. I gave her formula more and more and breastfed her less and less. While I was pregnant I had studied and committed to memory the benefits of breastfeeding. I even purchased the Rolls Royce of breast pumps: The Medela Pump In

Style backpack. It hadn't even been a month and already I'd shirked my responsibilities. As I shook the bottle I heard a voice chant, *You're giving your baby formula. If she gets cancer or isn't as smart as the other kids, it's because you didn't breastfeed her. You're giving your baby formula...*

I tried to sing "Itsy, Bitsy Spider" to her, but the chanting grew so loud that I screwed up the words, "down came the *brain* and washed the spider out..." and that set me off sobbing again. This time I couldn't stop. I called Chad and cried into the phone, then told him what I'd said to Isabelle that morning.

"You didn't mean it," he insisted. "You don't really hate her. Everyone knows that."

He left work anyway, called my obstetrician, and although I couldn't get in to see my regular doctor, he made an appointment with the doctor who'd delivered Isabelle. While we waited for Chad to get home, Isabelle was content as could be in her bouncy seat while I cried and pulled at my hair. If I'd known a way to unzip my skin and crawl outside of myself, I would have done it. I did know, though, in the tiniest chambers of my heart that I didn't hate my baby, and I spent the next ten minutes telling Isabelle how much I loved her, every single soft and sweet part of her. I tried to explain to her that mommy's emotions felt so crazy and that the hormonal fluctuations were making me a different person than the good mommy who was so focused and together when she was pregnant. Isabelle watched me with her big, brown eyes, spit up a few times, and let me rant and cry. It was especially hard to explain something to a one-month-old that I didn't understand myself.

* * *

When the doctor asked me what was wrong, I bawled. My symptoms: uncontrollable crying, indifference toward my new baby, lack of appetite, and insomnia. He said I was suffering from postpartum depression and recommended that I go back on the antidepressant. I was reluctant, but he insisted that postpartum depression was more common than many women let on, and he promised me that resuming the drug would help. I agreed to the lowest dose and he said that I would see an improvement in my mood within a week. A week seemed like an eon and I wondered if there was anything they could pipe into my veins for a more immediate effect. He then told me to take Benadryl that night to help me sleep. And as we were leaving, he slipped Chad the number to the clinic's mental health department and told him to schedule an appointment for me with a counselor. I snatched the business card from Chad's hand and shoved it into my purse.

That night I was convinced I wouldn't be able to sleep despite the fact that I had taken the Benadryl as directed. Even though Chad had to work in the morning, he'd offered to sleep in Isabelle's room and to feed her during the night so I wouldn't have to worry about getting up. But, as the hours ticked away, I became more and more agitated. I paced the floor in our bedroom and Chad eventually got up, calmed me down and sent me back to bed. I lay there as quietly as I could. He was in Isabelle's room, which was right next to ours, and I wanted him to be able to get some sleep so he would feel rested enough to go to work. I became obsessed with the idea of him getting enough sleep. Then I thought about the next day and the day after that, and how I didn't want to deal with any days. I buried my face in my pillow and screamed until my ears popped.

A few minutes later I heard Isabelle cry and I heard Chad get up to feed her. Guilt pummeled me and my body grew limp. I couldn't even take care of my own baby, and my husband was doing everything, plus working full time and going to school. My skin jumped to attention and started to crawl again. I sat up in bed, pulled at my hair and screamed into my pillow again and again, but there was no relief. I swung myself out of bed, hurried down the stairs, paced the kitchen for a few minutes, then grabbed my car keys. When I started my car, the clock radio said 2:23 a.m. Chad must have heard me open the garage door, because as I backed out of the driveway I saw him out of the corner of my eye. I pretended not to notice him.

"Call the police, you jerk," I hissed, my heart racing. "Maybe they'll lock me up somewhere and you won't have to deal with your crazy wife!"

In my hysteria, I knew I was losing it, and some part of me felt comforted by the fact that I was going crazy. My responsibilities were drifting away and I knew I wouldn't be held accountable for my actions anymore. Crazy people were never held accountable for their actions.

I looped around the small city again and again, no destination in mind and not too far from home—a crazy woman in pajamas and bare feet in a car full of vexation and voices. And it was somewhere around my umpteenth lap around the small downtown area that a feeling so awful inched up my spine, taking its time, then slithered over my shoulder and around my neck, gagging me with the weight of itself. I hunched over the steering wheel and became acutely aware of my shallow breathing. I closed my eyes for a split-second longer than I should have and it was in that instant that my mind was overwhelmed. I swerved to the side of the road with a poisonous realization: I wanted to die. No ifs, ands, or buts about it. My mind was the clearest it had been since giving birth to Isabelle. I wanted to die. Kill myself. It was the only way to get rid of this monster. I waited for the shock of realization to register, but there was no surprise in my eyes when I looked in the rearview mirror. Only a desperate, sickly woman who had lost all touch with reality.

It was just after three o'clock and I'd driven the same two-mile route for thirty-seven minutes. It was time to vary my course. As I approached the bridge, my heart thudded hard and consistently. I drove slowly, peering to my right. The moon, a full, glowing orb of promise, was reflected in the river and I saw the boat launch entrance off to the side. It would be so easy to drive into that swishing, swirling river and let everything go. I drove by the river two more times, envisioning my freedom, then finally headed home. Even at my worst I was a planner and I needed to plot my escape.

I passed the same cop for the third time and I wondered if I seemed suspicious to him. I seemed suspicious to myself. If he pulled me over I knew I would cry hysterically, and he would call the paramedics because I'd start hyperventilating again, and I'd try to tell him what was wrong, but it would all come out as a jumbled mess and that would get me a first-class ticket to the psych ward.

"Who the hell are you?" I shouted and the unfamiliar voice startled me. I looked in the rearview mirror again and it was me all right. The crazy woman who couldn't sit still, couldn't sleep, and didn't want anything to do with her baby.

Bad mother. Bad mother. Bad mother. The chanting in my head continued until I walked into our house, where Chad waited for me with a sleeping Isabelle in his arms. He was visibly worn out.

"Lay down with me in Isabelle's room," he instructed, and I followed him up the stairs. Out of exhaustion, I fell asleep for a few hours. When I awoke with a start, I forgot where I was for a millisecond, then felt physically choked by the awful beast that was still there, still lurking like a constrictive second skin. I wanted to scratch it off of me and, knowing that that wasn't normal, I started to cry again. I could tell Chad was overwhelmed. He left the room momentarily to shower and get ready for work while Isabelle slept in her bassinet. He returned to find me crouched on the bed, banging my head against the wall as I cried. I only know that I was banging my head against the wall from him later recounting the details of how frightened he was when he saw me in that state. What I remember is that he came into the room, asked me frantically why I was doing that, then held me tightly until I stopped sobbing.

Isabelle slept soundly through the whole episode, and downstairs Chad dug through my purse to find the number of the mental health counselor. He made an appointment for that day, and I sobbed at the kitchen table before we went because I felt guilty that he was missing another day of work.

"It doesn't matter," he assured me. "My boss understands."

How could he understand? I wanted to scream. *This isn't normal. I'm not normal.* Words failed me, though, and I cried.

"What's most important to me is that we get you better," he said.

"We don't even know what's wrong with me!" I said. "What is wrong with me?"

"We'll figure it out," Chad assured me, then kneeled next to me, one hand on my knee and one hand rubbing my back.

I nodded weakly and believed for a second that maybe I could get better, but then the creature plowed into me again, a not-so-subtle reminder that this thing, this terrible, monstrous thing, was stronger than me. Stronger than all of us put together.

Isabelle slept through the entire session with the counselor. I, on the other hand, cried for fifty-six minutes straight. Chad did most of the talking and the counselor, Jennifer, said we needed to call my OB as soon as we left to request a little "something-something" to help me sleep.

"Sleep disorders are the number one symptom of postpartum depression," she said, and insisted that the fact that I hadn't slept in two days, almost three, made me feel like I was losing my mind.

"I am losing my mind!" I urged, and Jennifer looked startled to hear me speak. She assured me that I wasn't the only mother to ever feel that way, but I didn't believe her. I was a sinking island and it was her job to tell me I could be saved. What did she care if I drove into the river or not? But Jennifer insisted that my main priority had to be to get a good night's sleep, and she didn't think when I was "slightly hysterical" that I could do that on my own.

In that moment I fully understood why sleep deprivation has been used as a form of torture. It did ease my mind a little to know that Jennifer didn't think I was crazy, but I was not happy about taking more drugs. It was a sign of weakness in my mind that I couldn't handle what was going on with my own body or take care of my own baby. It was frustrating to me that my family's history of anxiety and depression chose this time in my life to rear its ugly head.

Chad called the doctor who'd delivered Isabelle and gave him the instructions from the mental health counselor. He reluctantly prescribed a sleeping pill called Ambien but only ten days worth. He made it clear that the prescription would not be refilled. Ambien could become addictive, he told Chad and I wondered what I would do if I couldn't sleep on my own after ten days. I instantly dreaded the future and before I took the first pill I knew I was addicted.

I was so overwhelmed by the feelings I had that I decided to get a new journal to write down my thoughts. Writing had always been healing for me and it was traditionally the way I handled challenges. Often, if I could write my feelings down, then reread my words, it was easier for me to process my situation. However, when Chad and I went to Barnes and Noble that day, I found myself dumbfounded in the stationery section because I couldn't decide which journal to buy.

I stared at the rows of blank books and felt heaviness in my chest. It became hard for me to breathe and I knew the monster was back. In an instant, I crumpled to the floor and wept with my head heavy in my hands. Chad could have easily and understandably tried to avoid a scene by pulling me to my feet and hustling me out of the store. Or he could have ducked behind a rack and scurried to the magazine section at the other end of the building. He didn't, though. Instead he knelt down beside me and rubbed my back as shoppers exited quickly and avoided the section. Time elapsed. I don't know how much time, but I finally crawled to my feet and selected a hot pink spiral-bound journal with a pattern of funky flowers in purple, orange, green and blue. That journal, although brand new, was the only thing that reminded me of myself that day. I couldn't see myself in the mirror anymore, but in that journal's cover I saw the vibrant collage of wit and drama and bliss that I believed defined the real me.

I planned to fill the pages with words that would help me find my way back to that person.

I clutched my new book in my hands on the ride home while Chad talked to his mom on the phone. She planned to stay at our house that night to care for Isabelle so Chad and I could attempt to get a good night's sleep. I reluctantly took a full Ambien tablet and Chad came in to say goodnight to me fifteen minutes later. The little white tablet couldn't possibly work on me, I told Chad. But it did and I slept for nearly twelve hours. When I woke, I felt a pang of excitement. Refreshed and surprised.

I took the pill again the next night and slept for almost six hours before I lurched up in bed, wide awake. I felt foggy, but I didn't care about side effects. I was thrilled to have gotten some sleep and to glimpse the possibility that I had a shot at coming out the other side of whatever it was I was going through.

Chapter Four

I was in tears again. I lay in our bedroom and cried while Chad gave Isabelle a bottle, changed her diaper, and put her in her crib to watch her bear mobile. She loved her bears. Chad lay down by me in the bedroom and hugged me while I cried. He had arranged with work to take a family leave of absence due to my *condition* and he was running out of time. He was the store manager and I knew they could only find others to fill in for so long before they'd find another person to take his place for good. His boss, however, was extremely understanding and supportive of the situation. "A good, religious man," Chad called him.

"I don't want to upset you," Chad said and my mind flashed Code Red. He was about to divorce me. I knew it. Who the hell would want to be married to a crazy woman like me? I didn't even want to be around me.

I turned to face him. "But?" I asked and the tears that had been on standby spilled out of my eyes.

"How would you feel about me calling your mom to see if she'd come here for a little bit to help us out?"

And then you'd divorce me? I wanted to ask, but I became preoccupied with the idea of my mother coming up from Florida again. At first I was furious with Chad for even suggesting I needed my mom to take care of me, but then I thought it might be a good idea, and a split-second later I felt guilty that I had disrupted everyone's lives with my psychosis. Guilt seemed to be my main companion.

I flat out refused to ask for any help and I would not be the one to call my mother, I told Chad. If Chad felt like calling her, fine, but I was not the one asking for help. Plain and simple.

Chad did call my mom that afternoon while I sat on the deck making a mental list of the things I had to do that weren't getting done. It was the end of April and I had myself convinced I would never get my vegetable garden planted or do the seasonal landscaping I enjoyed so much. Even if I had the time, I didn't have the energy and I really didn't care. I didn't care about the little things, the big things, or anything in between. Chad interrupted my destructive thoughts when he sat down next to me.

"She wants you to call her," he said as he held out his phone.

"What'd she say?" I asked without looking up. I was embarrassed that he had to call my mom. I was thirty-one and couldn't even take care of myself. Or even better, I was thirty-one and too much for my husband to take care of. Who was the baby here?

"She's going to talk to her manager tomorrow and see how soon she can get here," Chad said.

"She's coming?" I asked, and heard a twinge of hope in my voice. When things went wrong, which they rarely did, I really believed Mom could fix it. She had the gift.

* * *

I saw the counselor again the next Wednesday. I was absolutely beside myself because I couldn't sleep on my own without the Ambien. I obsessed about the stupid little pills and when that got old I obsessed about the fact that I was obsessing about the stupid little pills. I told Jennifer that I only had two pills left, so she made an appointment with Dr. Daily the next day who she said would prescribe me more sleeping pills.

Thursday, May 3

Today is a bad day. I hate my life today. No specific part of my life, just the whole thing. I feel so awful that I just want to throw up. I can't even explain the feeling, but it's gagging me. Like a giant finger down my throat. Poke. Poke. Poke.

It doesn't matter that I have a healthy daughter, a wonderful husband, and that Mom's coming tomorrow. None of that makes this horrible feeling go away. It's days like today that make me wonder how I'm going to get to tomorrow. Through tomorrow. Or if I even want to see tomorrow. What's waiting there that could make me care?

I saw Dr. Daily today and she upped my dose of the antidepressant and gave me more Ambien. She asked me if I'd thought about killing myself and I said yes. She didn't even flinch, typed in a note on the computer and went on to the next question: "Do you use tobacco?" Apparently admitting that I WANT TO DIE is not a cause for alarm. Maybe the sign to watch for is a patient who says no, then looks away mysteriously. Maybe people who really want to kill themselves aren't honest.

I almost got hit by a UPS truck when I walked out of the clinic. The driver wasn't watching where he was going and stopped abruptly, his tires making an annoyed squeak at me. I didn't make much effort to get out of the way, and after he left, I stood in the parking lot, wishing for several seconds that he would have hit me. That's not fair to anyone, but I did think it and even thought about it later, and right now, I don't think it's such a bad idea.

Mom arrived on Friday and I tried to put on a happy face. She was used to the chatty daughter who had a million things to say about nothing, not this empty shell of a person who stared blankly at the wall looking for comfort in eggshell white paint. The hopeful part of me, tiny as it was, believed I would feel better with Mom around, even if it was a fake-it-till-I-feel-it scenario.

The counselor and doctor had both demanded that I put everything work related aside for at least four weeks. I reluctantly agreed while in the back of my mind I reassured myself that they had no way of knowing if I checked my e-mail or scribbled down some ideas for the magazine. Mom cooked and cleaned and did everything and anything she could think of to take the pressure off of me. But I still felt wound tight as a yo-yo. I spent a lot of time that weekend with Isabelle, and with my doctor's consent, I started breastfeeding her again. I even thought I could make counselor Jennifer proud by creating a list of all of the wonderful aspects of my life. Unfortunately I couldn't convince myself to care enough to think about it, let alone get a piece of paper.

Mom and I agreed that it might be a good idea to put Isabelle in day care a couple of days a week when she turned six weeks old. I rationalized that it would give me some time alone to ease back into life, then back into work. I called dozens of numbers in the newspaper and numbers listed on our county's Web site, but there were no openings. Every person asked when my baby would be born, and when I told them she was already here, they acted like I'd announced that I liked to pull out her tiny baby hairs one by one.

"Oh!" one woman exclaimed. "You're calling now? Don't you know that there are waiting lists for day care? Most women call when they're pregnant to set that up…"

"Oh—" was all I could get out before she continued.

"It would have been a good idea to call during your first trimester," she cheerfully added.

I clicked off the phone before I threw it at the wall. "Ahhhh!" I screamed and Mom rushed into the room.

"Apparently normal parents who have a clue about what they're doing also have the foresight to make day care arrangements during their pregnancy," I said. "And I guess the smart ones go on some sort of interview process with the top three."

Mom sat down across from me. "I heard about Linda from a friend and signed you up after you were born."

I rolled my eyes. Linda was our "sitter," as she called herself, and was the epitome of laziness in a tiny apartment. Rainy days were the worst when we couldn't get out of the smoke-filled living room where Linda slugged down bottle after bottle of Pepsi and subjected us to a back-to-back litany of soap operas. It didn't matter if *He-Man, Smurfs,* or *Scooby-Doo* were on another channel. It was Linda's house and we went by Linda's rules. She could always be found on the floral-patterned, harvest-gold and avocado-green kitchen chair she'd put in the living room by the sliding glass door. From her second-floor perch she could see all the goings-on outside and still catch every last one of Victor's moves on *All My Children.*

We, the children at Linda's, were an afterthought. When an odor wafted by her nose, she ordered the diapered kids to line up in front of her while she plunged two fingers down the back of their pants. When she found the source, she directed one of the older kids to change the diaper. I avoided eye contact during this ritual and tried to sink deeper into whatever book I was reading. I was usually the one summoned to do her dirty work. But that wasn't the worst part. The worst part was that she rarely got up to wash her hands after the search was done.

I didn't want that for Isabelle.

In Mom's defense, she worked full time and basically did everything for us kids while Dad did the typical guy stuff—such as mowing the grass and fixing the cars. On the outside, Linda's probably didn't look so bad to Mom, especially since we were instructed by Linda not to go home "tattlin'" when something bad happened. And, despite the list that ran through my head every so often of mildly traumatizing experiences at Linda's (being shot by a BB gun at close range, run over by one of her sons on a bicycle, and clubbed in the temple with a baseball bat that left me with blurred vision for two days), in the grand scheme of things, it probably wasn't that bad.

Yet, with all of those strikes against Linda's place, I still preferred the idea of an in-home day care to a commercial establishment. Well, actually, Superwoman hadn't planned to put Isabelle in day care at all, but slackers couldn't be choosers. Finally, I broke down and Mom and I made an appointment to tour a KinderCare Center less than two miles away. There was nothing overly comforting about the place, but nothing glaringly awful either. Out of desperation, I agreed to Tuesdays and Thursdays beginning in mid-May to the tune of $175 per week. And with that quick calculation, my money worries started all over again.

I sank like a brick into a pool of guilt and dripped with disgrace when I tried to pull myself out. *How the hell did other moms do this?*

I spent that afternoon entertaining myself with images of breaking down completely—running out into the backyard screaming in the pouring rain, flopping to the floor in the middle of Target while picking up diapers, planting my face into the salad my mother so lovingly prepared. They all seemed like good options. That night, I visualized throwing myself off of the roof, but since we only had a two-story house with a basement, the best I could hope for was a broken limb and internal bleeding. I went to bed that night while Chad and Mom watched a movie downstairs with Isabelle. I was overcome with dread. Again. Thick like the proverbial quicksand I felt I was sinking into. I took an Ambien, lay down, and marveled at the horrific thoughts racing through my head, thoughts I never imagined I could have. I tried to write them down, but my hand felt crippled and my pen seemed to weigh a thousand pounds.

Monday, May 7

I thought I was doing better with Mom here, but I feel so awful right now that I don't want to live another minute. I don't know what to do. I can't stop crying. Chad is totally frustrated with me and has just about had it with me. He hasn't said that, but I can tell.

I don't know what to do.
I don't know what to do.
I don't know what to do.
I don't know what to do.
I don't know what to do.
I don't know what to do.
I don't know what to do.
I don't know what to do.
I don't know what to do.
I don't know what to do.
I can't do this anymore. My skin is crawling.

Dear Isabelle,

I'm so sorry. It might not seem like it now, but things will be better for you. Life is hard enough, Isabelle, and the last thing you need is a crazy mommy. I'm not doing you any good and I'm not getting any better. Your daddy will take good care of you and he's got a big family to help him.

Don't worry about your daddy, he's a lot stronger than even he realizes. He can make you smile just by walking by you and he takes care of you every night when I can't. He knows when you're tired and hungry just by your cries, and he loves you so much.

Some day you will undoubtedly question why I would leave you if I claim to love you so much. I can't handle the pressure and stress I'm putting on your daddy and the terrible way I'm feeling. Please don't ever think it was because of you. You're an angel, and I don't want to expose you to mommy's bad days.

You're so young now that other people will quickly fill the void I leave and I think the whole circle will be stronger because of it. I'm a weak link.

I want you to know… Here are some of my favorite things about you:

When I read over my journal entry the next day, I realized the Ambien took effect and I fell asleep in the middle of my sentence. At first I wanted to tear the page out of my journal. I didn't, though. Over the next two days the feeling that I needed to *leave* came on stronger and stronger, and it actually comforted me to know I had an option. I didn't have to suffer anymore. I didn't feel like counseling could even begin to chip away at this monster that had taken up residence inside of me. And the drugs, they just weren't working. The only light at the end of the tunnel was that I could be the one to let it all go.

Isabelle's baptism was scheduled for Sunday and I made a deal with myself that I had an obligation to her to attend her baptism, to be there when she was formally inducted into God's family. When she got older, just like me, she could make her own choices about God and religion.

After the baptism you are free to do what you need to do, I told myself. It was Thursday and Sunday seemed too far away.

Thursday, May 10

Something propelled me today to tell Chad about my "bad" thoughts and he told my mother. I guess the fact that I told him I want to die could mean I really don't. Sometimes it just feels good to know there's an option to make all of this awful stuff go away.

I do have to say that I'm surprised my thought process has gone in this direction, but I'm not going to censor myself because it's taboo to talk about killing yourself.

Mom and Chad both demanded that I never think about that again. How stupid is that? How stupid are they? It reminded me of confirmation. "Never question the Bible." "Never question God's teachings."

I can't promise that I won't have thoughts that I can't control. I have lost control. Sometimes I dip so low that getting out of this awful world is the only thing I can think about.

For the next couple of days I tried to pretend I was feeling better and was careful with my movements. I didn't want to do anything that might be construed as "suicidal behavior." Saturday morning I decided I couldn't make it to Sunday, not even to attend Isabelle's baptism. Chad and Mom diligently prepared for the celebration. Our dog, Raven, looked especially scraggly and Chad suggested she have a haircut. I volunteered to take her and Mom looked at me with a shocked expression.

"Really?" she asked, washing the fruit that she'd cut up for a fruit salad. She was so good at preparing for events. So efficient.

I shrugged, then clipped Raven's leash to her collar.

"Well, it might be good for you to get out," she said without looking up.

I'm hoping I'll get into a fatal accident, I wanted to say, but I didn't. She probably wouldn't have let me go.

I dropped Raven off at Petco for her grooming appointment, and on my way home I drove down by the river, the swishing-swirling fast-paced Minnesota River, then proceeded down to the boat launch. I let my front tires touch the water and waited to feel appalled at myself. I felt nothing. Instead I got mad that I didn't have the guts to do it already. I was responsible in my thinking. I didn't want to drive the whole car into the river. There was value in my Jeep and Chad could use the money when I was gone. But would I have the guts to wade in and keep going until my toes could no longer touch the bottom? Until the water lapped just below my mouth? Would I have the guts to let go and allow the water to swish away this demon that wouldn't let me be? It was clear I couldn't get rid of it without getting rid of myself.

When I got home I told Mom and Chad I was going to lay down. I didn't lay down, though. I went through a box of my favorite things. Chad jokingly called it my "Hope Chest" the first time he saw the wood box with a sailboat decoupaged on top. I collected pictures of my sister and me, a scrap of paper Chad gave me when we first started dating (on which he listed his name as "The Man of My Dreams" and his phone number), a cross necklace with an emerald in the center Mom gave me for my confirmation, a heart Dad had cut out of metal during a welding class, and other trinkets from my childhood. I put the items in a plastic bag so they wouldn't get wet, then went into my office to a filing cabinet where I kept our personal information. I took out my life insurance policy and a folder where I kept all of our important contacts, as well as the Web sites and passwords to pay our bills online. I set the papers on my desk in plain view. Chad would need those things and this would all be hard enough on him without having to search high and low for the details of our life.

That afternoon when I went back to Petco I was absolute in my thinking. I was aware of my transition into a trancelike state. I'd made my plan, took care of the details, and was ready to act. I would collect Raven and on the way home I would drive to the river, park my car, crack the windows slightly so the dog wouldn't overheat, then I would wade into the water until it rushed over my head. The current would be strong enough to wash me away. Even if I fought it, I would be in over my head. Eventually the struggle would wear me out and I would surrender. The fight would finally be over.

Raven would be fine in the car until someone found her. The weather was warm, but it wasn't hot. Nonetheless, I brought a small bowl and a container of water for her. I would park in the shade of a small maple tree. She had a blue collar with a name tag, so anyone wondering why she was in the car alone would be able to call Chad. I'd leave the doors unlocked.

I imagined my escape with vivid detail while I waited at the stoplight to turn into the parking lot of Petco. And it was during that wait that a softball-sized sphere of shocking numbness blasted through my windshield and into the pit of my stomach, radiating with tingling tentacles up into my chest, along my arms, and into my face. All at once, it pounded on my heart, gripped my throat, and scratched the air out of me. I knew it wasn't the beast. It was lighter, brighter and a hell of a lot stronger. The stoplight turned green and I found the wherewithal to inch across the intersection to the parking lot, a sense of vertigo blurring my vision. My body shook and my breathing came in short gasps, but I made it to the other side of the road.

"Oh…my…god," I gasped through tight teeth. "I'm going to die. I'm going to friggin' die right here!"

Somehow I parked my car and dug through my purse for my cell phone to call Chad. He always calmed me when I had bouts of anxiety, but this was clearly more than an anxiety attack. This was the death I longed for spiraling around inside of me. I could see my fingers, but they didn't look like my fingers as the hands they were connected to rooted around in my purse. I couldn't find my phone. The realization that I had left my phone at home made my heart slam in my chest: *Thud. Thud. Thud.* I looked down and actually saw my skin bounce with each thunderous pump. Had anyone's heart actually burst out of their chest before?

Kaboom, kaboom, kaboom! The pounding moved to my ears. My hands and feet shook violently, but I managed to swing the car door open and fall to a half-in, half-out position. Every cell in my body was on high alert. Vomit burned in my throat. My face buzzed, my lips tingled, and my stomach leaped. I closed my eyes for what felt like an eternity, and when I came to I was able to slide back into my seat. The dash clock told me the whole ordeal had only lasted about three minutes. With a shaking foot, I moved my car to a spot in front of Petco's grooming entrance. Somehow I propelled myself inside. I wanted to hold Raven, to feel the comfort of her familiarity. I felt light, like I weighed four pounds rather than 140, and I knew in that instant that something larger than a panic attack had hit me.

Raven leaped up behind the counter like she was spring loaded. She was so excited to see me, even though it had only been three hours—and I was surprised at my excitement to see her. I led her by her leash to a small hill at the edge of the parking lot and sat down. I hugged her so hard that she gave a little yelp, but quickly licked my face to let me know it was nothing personal. She smelled like musky dog cologne.

"I don't think I want to die, Raven," I said and buried my face in her black fur. "I don't want to leave you, and daddy, and Isabelle! I don't want to die!"

I cried until I was out of breath again, and I'm sure anyone watching me thought I was either a nut case or very unhappy with my dog's haircut. Either way, it was the first time in weeks that I felt alive.

"I don't want to die," I whispered again as I petted Raven, "but I don't know what to do."

As we walked to the car, the gray cloud seemed to shift ever so slightly and my mind drifted into unfamiliar territory, like I was a kite without a string. Up there, above it all, I was able to glimpse a future, and I felt nervous and a little excited about where my thoughts were heading.

Raven hopped onto the passenger's seat and I slid into the driver's seat. I folded my hands in front of me, closed my eyes, and in a whisper, I asked God to help me.

Chapter Five

It wasn't all sunshine and roses after my prayer, and, to be truthful, I felt deeply disappointed in God. Again. I tried to be patient and believe it was him that tricked me into deciding not to kill myself, but I wasn't convinced.

Saturday, May 12

It's 8:30 p.m. and I'm going to bed. I'm hoping the extra sleep will help me. Tomorrow is Isabelle's baptism, and on Monday Mom leaves to go back to Florida. I want to get better. I don't want to have bad thoughts anymore. I know this is going to be hard and I won't feel better overnight. Somehow, though, when I'm in the midst of the awful "spells" that make me think about horrible things like taking my own life, I have to believe it will get better.

I've been angry at God for not helping me when I've asked for his help. Of course I haven't always been real pleasant with my requests, but I do have to give him some credit, I guess. He has given me the unconditional love of Chad and Mom. He has given me Isabelle.

I've been mad because I asked him to help me sleep, but I couldn't sleep. But if I look at things differently, I was connected with a doctor who gave me Ambien, which helps me to sleep. I even went so far the other day as to yell at God and tell him I don't believe in him anymore, but maybe the simple fact that I'm yelling at him means I do believe. One look at Isabelle and I believe.

The day of Isabelle's baptism was also Mother's Day, and Chad surprised me with a gold mother and daughter charm on a gold chain. I actually felt like a mother that day, and not such a bad one either,

41

and I proudly displayed the emblem around my neck. I dressed in one of my favorite black skirts with embroidered flowers near the trim, a pink shirt, and matching pink shoes.

I started calling Isabelle "Izzy" that day. The nickname suited her when she was in her joyful moods, her arms and legs kicking every which way. I liked that I had a nickname for her. I didn't care that other people had been calling her Izzy for weeks. Good moms had nicknames for their little ones and I hoped I was on the right track.

Isabelle was an absolute angel during her baptism. Awake through the whole ceremony, she posed like a princess when Pastor Tom carried her up and down the aisles to show off "Cross of Peace's newest child of God." Truthfully, it all seemed like a play and acting to me: the special dress, blessing her with holy water, and having the entire church recite a script that pledged their support for her spiritual journey. Would God really have thought less of her if I had denied her this ceremony? Did this ritual even matter? A small part of me guessed it probably did, especially to the family members and friends sitting in the pews. I wished it mattered more to me.

When Pastor Tom gently handed Isabelle back to me, I wondered if my little girl would be better than her mother at following the rules of the church. I wanted her to be better and to have that connection to God and the support of a church behind her, especially since I hadn't had those things. It would be good for her.

* * *

Mom left for Florida the next morning and I went to the library and checked out the book *Down Came the Rain* by Brooke Shields about her struggle with postpartum depression. I set it on the coffee table and glanced at it every time I walked by. I wasn't ready to crack the spine. The book was still glossy and new and it didn't look like anyone had even checked it out, let alone read it.

The next day I brought Isabelle to KinderCare at 8 a.m.

"Hello," one of the teenagers said as I walked into the room with Isabelle, strapped into her car seat, and the labeled bottles I was required to bring.

"Here's Isabelle," I said, and tried to act like a cheery new mom who maybe had some small problems but definitely not anything big like suicidal tendencies and severe postpartum depression.

"Who?" another girl asked, flipping through some papers.

The maternal part of me wanted to scoop Isabelle and her bottles up and get the hell out of there pronto, but another girl had already pulled my baby out of her car seat and another was putting her bottles into the fridge.

"Okay," the girl said and pushed the car seat aside. "We'll take good care of her."

I couldn't will my feet to move. "Do you want my number or something in case you have to call me?"

"We'll find it," she offered between snaps of her gum. "You filled out the registration form, right?"

Isabelle stared at me as the girl held her with one arm and my baby's little lips curled up in a smile.

"Let me give you my number anyway," I said, and scribbled the digits on a napkin. I waved it her way then placed it on top of the microwave. "I'll have my phone on me all day."

The girl gave me the courtesy of a smile. She probably thought I was just another nervous mom and I thought maybe she was right. I hadn't had my head on right since the day Isabelle was born, and somehow I found the momentum to cruise out of the place before I could change my mind. When I got home I felt disoriented and sick to my stomach. *I should go back and get her,* I thought. *But then I'd have to take care of her all day.* I didn't think I had the energy to do that. Still, I felt terrible that my six-week-old was in someone else's care and I didn't have anything pressing to do—such as go to work.

I called twice before 10 a.m. and finally settled down by noon with Brooke Shields' book. I wasn't even a quarter of the way through the book when relief spilled out of my eyes that someone, anyone, knew how I felt. And it seemed that Brooke considered postpartum depression to be a real medical condition. Of course, our situations were very different. I didn't have a nanny for Isabelle and no one cooked our family meals, but the helpless lethargy and desire to escape linked us in a secret tribe of women that Brooke called PPD Survivors. She gave statistics and resources at the back of her book and I was astounded to learn how many women experience the phenomenon of intense hormonal fluctuations, racing thoughts, and lack of sleep. I felt driven to learn more, to find women locally who were experiencing what I was experiencing. Before I could make a plan, Chad arrived home early and we drove together to pick up Isabelle.

"I had a good day," I told him as we pulled into the establishment's parking lot. I was proud to say those words, and Chad smiled at me and patted my leg.

There were children running wild when we entered the building and I feared the worst. I could tell from the way Chad grabbed my hand that he was afraid, too. We hustled down the hallway to the infants' room and when we pushed through the doorway at the same time, I spotted Isabelle immediately, comfortably curled into the curve of a Boppie pillow. She lay contently, mesmerized by her own tiny hand. I slapped my hand to my chest and exhaled a sigh of relief. Chad and I exchanged a look and I knew in an instant that we couldn't bring her back there, even though she appeared to be fine.

Coincidentally, when we got home I received a call from Carla Olson, who provided day care services out of her home just a few miles away. She had an opening. We scheduled an appointment with her for the next evening, which would be right after we attended the postpartum support group Chad found online.

Wednesday, May 16

I'm so glad to report that the support group seemed helpful. I was worried that I wouldn't be able to identify with anyone or that I would be the most extreme postpartum case they'd ever seen. I was surprised that there were only three other girls in the meeting room and that it's the only PPD group in the Twin Cities area.

All three talked about sleeping troubles and one recalled that there was a time she didn't sleep for eight days straight. She had been a mess, hospitalized and everything, and I realized that maybe I wasn't the worst case ever.

I told "my story" and I really felt like they knew what I was talking about. I think it was good for Chad, too. I know how lucky I am to have him, but I felt especially thankful today when the other girls talked about their husbands, wishing that they'd come to a meeting like Chad did. I'm glad I have his support since he was cognizant enough to recognize the postpartum depression in the first place.

I'm not ready to say out loud that I'm feeling better. I have gone two days without crying—this is a big deal in my world—but I still feel like I'm teetering on the edge, like I'm waiting for the ball to drop and take me with it.

The group of girls, and the lady running the show, seemed to think my sleep would improve as I start to feel better and my antidepressant fully kicks in. I'm looking forward to that. Sleeping has always been a favorite pastime of mine and I miss it.

A few days later, Chad's mom watched Isabelle and I went to a meeting for the magazine. It was refreshing to have adult conversations. I felt alive again and caught snippets of my old self. We talked about a feature story and I was energized with ideas for sidebars and a graphic. As I got into my car I realized that, during the two-hour meeting, I hadn't thought once about "my condition." I felt good so I decided to go to the real estate office to sift through my mail. When I got there, though, my mood immediately turned and I had an unnaturally irritated reaction to the idea of talking to any buyers or sellers.

I called Mom to wish her a happy birthday and tried to express to her how much her support meant to me, then I launched into a tirade.

"I hate real estate," I said. "I don't want to do it anymore."

"Everyone has bad days," she said, and I clenched my teeth. She couldn't begin to understand my bad days.

"Yes, they do," I agreed and tried to focus on my gratitude for our close relationship.

"I pray that Isabelle and I will have the kind of relationship we do," I told her before I wished her a final happy birthday and hung up.

I was still surprised that Mom's presence hadn't immediately snapped me out of the postpartum depression. She'd always been able to fix everything from stinging slivers to holes in my favorite jeans. But this was beyond her control and I imagined that watching me curled into the fetal position at thirty-one years of age might have been a little hard on her, too.

When I got home my energy level was still higher than it had been for weeks, so I went to the gym and walked on the treadmill for 30 minutes. I wondered if I was finally on the upswing. Or maybe I'd become bipolar in the process and I was headed for my high before I tanked again.

Monday, May 21

I've only taken half a sleeping pill the last three nights. I had a good weekend—at least good by today's standards. I didn't cry or imagine throwing myself out of a window, so I consider that an improvement. Still, I feel like that awful monster is right there, not in me anymore but only a few feet away, ready to strike again and knock me on my butt. The slightest bit of sadness worries me that everything's going to dip south again.

I brought Isabelle to a picnic at the real estate office today. I had to show her off. She'll be eight weeks old tomorrow and she's growing so fast! I wish I could say it was nice to see everyone at the picnic, but I was honestly glad to get back into the privacy of my own car with my little girl. I didn't want to listen to competing stories about the fussiest buyers, or the tales from the ever-popular gloating agent who cackled about "how easy this business really is once you learn how to read people."

The gathering made me wish I could make a better living freelance writing. Journalists and writers aren't paid nearly enough for their talents, yet business execs (or real estate agents, for that matter) often make gajillions simply by telling people what they want to hear. I guess that's a talent in some arenas. But are those people passionate about what they do? Maybe. Or maybe they don't ask the tough questions like, "What am I really on this planet to do anyway? What is my gift to the world?" Maybe they just go to work, do their job, and go home like good mommies and daddies. Maybe that's what I'm supposed to do.

I'm passionate about writing and have been for as long as I can remember, but is that a good enough reason to have my income drop by half? Chad would say no. Our creditors would say no. So I continue to stare blankly at the wall doing nothing, because I just don't know.

Chapter Six

I listened to the Bee Gees while I was pregnant with Isabelle. I've had a thing for the trio of falsetto fellows since my mother introduced them to me as a child. Not in person, unfortunately, but via eight track. Their *Greatest Hits* album was my strongest craving during my pregnancy, and the music gave me a high that I'm pretty sure wasn't just my hormones. Apparently Isabelle liked them, too. By eight weeks, she responded to the Bee Gees better than she did to my voice. If she fussed and my mood was okay, I swayed in front of her to "How Deep Is Your Love." And if we were having a particularly difficult evening, Chad slid into the kitchen and boogied to "Night Fever." She stared, not smiling, not crying, just fixated on us like this was a circus and we were her clowns. The Bee Gees were our thing and they travelled everywhere with us that summer.

By mid-July I could tell the postpartum depression was lifting. I continued to attend the support group on Wednesdays and, at the most recent one, watched a longtime member, Lydia, break down completely. The director recommended that she admit herself to a two-week day program during which doctors would analyze the different medications she was on—a concoction of pills for sleeping, anxiety, and depression—then offer her intensive therapy sessions and get her on the right path to recovery, since her current path signaled disaster in the director's mind. It was scary to see her that way. Judging from the looks on the other girls' faces, I think we each believed it could have been any one of us slumped in our chair, barely able to speak. We all saw ourselves in Lydia.

I thought on the way home that if I had gone to that support group on one of my worst days—maybe the day I brought Raven to Petco—the director might have insisted on that program for me, too. My passion for writing poked at me until I started freelancing again for the newspaper. Isabelle was in day care at Carla's house three days a week and I had more time to work. At the end of the day, I longed for my little girl and could barely control my excitement during the four-minute drive to Carla's house. Seeing her lying on a blanket in the grass with the other kids running around her made my heart sing. And when she spotted me and burst into the crooked grin we called her "Elvis smile," I knew we were meant for each other.

I updated the Web site for my melted bottle craft business, while real estate remained in the back of my mind. Even with my improved mood I still didn't feel like I could make real estate work for me. The only thing I enjoyed about the business was making eye-catching brochures to stuff in the spider-infested boxes that perched atop "for sale" signs, or brainstorming creative headlines for the Sunday open house ads. Those tasks didn't pay the bills, and each month Chad and I continued to hemorrhage money from our savings account.

I told my friend Marti that I thought often about expanding my craft business and she offered to come with me to a business class at WomenVenture in Minneapolis. She thought she might like to open a dog bakery someday. I had run the numbers and knew that in order to make a decent living I'd have to sell at least 1,500 bottles per year. The time commitment hadn't bothered me before. Melting glass was one of my crafty hobbies and I enjoyed making cool stuff from old junk. One of my fears with expanding Daisy Glass was that I would become so overwhelmed by orders for the bottles that it wouldn't be fun for me anymore. I liked the idea of running my own business and having my own schedule. That's what appealed to me about real estate. I wasn't convinced, though, that expanding Daisy Glass was the answer and I started to wonder if I'd ever find my direction.

With Isabelle, though, I finally felt like we were getting into a routine. She spent the weekend with Chad's mom while Chad and I went to a friend's wedding, then we met up with Chad's family on Sunday for dinner at a Japanese restaurant called "Kami." Isabelle was an absolute angel. She watched the chef with great intensity as he created large flames in front of us, and she snuggled next to me while we waited for our food. She was content when she drifted off to sleep that night, too, so I was surprised to be woken at 2 a.m. by her crying. It had been weeks since she'd woken up during the night, and some mornings I had to go into her room at nine or ten o'clock to rouse her because she was still snoozing—a trait she must have picked up from her daddy.

I tried to give her a bottle, but she wasn't hungry. Instead, she was wide awake and wanted to play. Even though I was tired, I had to accommodate her. She was so darn cute and her little personality was making me love her more and more every day. I brought her downstairs, got myself a snack, came back up, and changed her diaper. I played with her toes and did her favorite exercise where I pulled on her arms and she used all of her girly muscles to pull herself to a sitting position. Usually this involved grunting and sticking out her tongue. It only took ten minutes of gentle rocking to her *Baby Nursery Rhymes* CD and she was off to dreamland again.

I went back to bed and didn't wake up until just after nine. I was sleeping better, my patience had returned, and I finally felt like Isabelle and I were bonding. I sneaked into her room and she was already awake, legs wiggling around as she gazed up at her bear mobile. When she saw me, her face lit up and I felt truly amazed by my daughter.

It was the kind of sunny day people wish for: no clouds, the tiniest breeze, and the thick smell of summer in the air. I thought about playing hooky and I considered calling Carla to tell her Isabelle would be absent from day care because we had big plans to lounge around and stare at the cloudless sky for most of the afternoon. But as I gave her a bath and she splashed and splashed, my mind turned to swimming lessons and water toys, then bicycles, letter jackets, and, eventually, bills for college tuition. I remembered Dad's offhand comments when my sister and I were growing up about how our financial requests were "draining his savings" and "sucking him dry," but he never failed to provide for us everything we needed and most of what we wanted. I would do the same for Isabelle. And with that thought, responsibility won out. This was the day I would figure out what I would do with myself from a work perspective.

Isabelle was hilarious, "my little gigglebox," I called her as I picked out her clothes. She was too big for the first outfit I tried on her, so I dressed her in a purple and white sundress, then lay her on the bathroom rug while I brushed my teeth. I could see in the mirror that she was watching me, and when I turned quickly to make a face at her, she let out an ear-piercing squeal of delight. She had recently found her voice and was full of the squeaks and screeches that were music to my ears.

We strolled into day care at 10 a.m., and I was struck with pride when one of the other little girls ran up to us and yelled, "Isabelle's here!" My little princess was already making friends and she wasn't even four months old. I wondered if she would be that girl like me in school that didn't fit into one specific clique, but was friends with just about everybody.

When I left Carla's, I drove aimlessly through our city's small downtown area, trying to decide which way to go. I couldn't bear the thought of going into the real estate office, so I poked around in the library until noon, researching the basics of starting my own business. I ran the numbers again and wondered if I was being a complete idiot. At what point did people just bite the bullet and work, even if they didn't feel *fulfilled?* Was work really satisfying to anyone? My parents had the same jobs for thirty-some years and never would have thought about dabbling in something else to see if they enjoyed themselves more. There was no security in dabbling. They believed you worked five days a week without complaining and enjoyed yourself in the evenings and on the weekends. *That* forty hours, though, that wasn't yours. It belonged to *The Man* and you had no right to complain. You were lucky to have a job, to be able to support your family and to have a roof over your head. So, was it my age group, on the cusp of Generation X, nearly Generation Y, that had such horrendous entitlement issues? What was up with the constant uneasiness and the ever-present desire to "find myself"?

Looking back at my first real estate transaction three years earlier, I never did feel that real estate was my "calling." Selling houses was a way to potentially make a lot of money and, at the time I went through the classes and got my license, money equaled happiness for me. Maybe money wasn't the cure-all for life's problems, but it made a great Band-aid, and, from my perspective, a wad of cash had the ability to take away the sting of just about any wound.

Oh, but there was something about that little girl of mine. She was screwing with all of my preconceived notions of what I wanted to do with my life. Wealth and a lakeside home slipped to the bottom of my priority ladder and spending time with my family shot up to the top rung. My creativity level for writing and creating art was at an all-time high.

When I got home from the library a couple of hours later I felt absolutely wiped out from the brainpower it took to try to determine my life's new path. I did set a new goal, though, to do everything work-wise during the days when Isabelle was at day care, so I could devote myself 100 percent in the evenings to Chad and Isabelle—easier said than done in the nights and weekends world of real estate.

I lay down to take a short nap and I glanced at the clock, 1:45 p.m., thinking it could take me all afternoon to fall asleep. The phone rang at 2 p.m. on the dot and I thought for a brief second about not answering. I was tired of telemarketers trying to sell me on the Scam du Jour. Chad called every day from work, though, so I answered in hopes that it would be him "just calling to say hi."

"Amy!" he shouted in the voice he used when he wanted to get my attention. "Isabelle's being airlifted to Children's Hospital. She stopped breathing."

"What?" I cried. *But is she breathing now? Did she have a toy in her mouth?* "What happened? What's wrong? Is she okay?"

Chad blurted something about Children's Hospital and directions, then we hung up. My mind was freakishly clear as I hustled down the stairs, grabbed my purse and keys, and slipped into my flip-flops. I even had the clarity to choose my black flip-flops over my tan ones since they matched better with my jeans and black tank top. When I pulled out of the driveway my mind clicked into high gear. This was a crisis situation and, suddenly, no rules applied to me. I needed to get to the hospital and I need to get there *immediately*. Unfortunately, the drive was at least half an hour, but I was determined to cut that time in half as I sped through stop signs, around cars, and onto the freeway in my Jeep Liberty that coughed and hissed whenever I hit the gas too hard.

I dialed my sister's number first knowing she always had her cell phone handy. No answer. My sister-in-law, Jennie, called and said Chad had just called her.

"I'm on my way over to pick you up," she said, her voice frantic. She only lived a few blocks away from us.

"I'm already on the freeway," I said, then hung up and called Mom.

Mom was at work, 2,000 miles away. As I told her what I knew, which wasn't much, I became more and more agitated.

"Hang up the phone and concentrate on driving," she demanded, always overly concerned with my driving. "Call me when you get to the hospital."

Then I called 911 and told the operator I was in a blue Jeep on Highway 169 and I was speeding. "My daughter is being airlifted to Children's in Minneapolis," I told the woman.

"Stay on the line," she said in a flat voice. She connected me to a sheriff, who informed me he couldn't authorize me to speed.

"Then can you authorize your officers not to pull me over?" I asked, desperate for compassion.

He was silent for a moment. "If they do pull you over just tell them what's happening."

"Oh, I won't be pulling over," I said, glancing down at the speedometer needle hovering at 90. "You can either tell them to follow me or lead me, but I won't be pulling over."

"Ma'am, I can't authorize you to speed," he said again.

"Okay," I said, hung up the phone and adjusted my speed from 90 to 85. I couldn't stand the silence in the car. I couldn't stand not knowing what was happening with Isabelle. I dialed Chad's cell phone number. He was on his way to the hospital from work and quickly settled me down.

"The last thing I need is to have my daughter *and* my wife in the hospital," he said, so I resigned myself to 75 miles per hour.

I disconnected with Chad, stayed off the shoulder, and only honked at slow drivers a few more times before arriving 25 minutes later in Minneapolis. Once on city streets, I kicked into high gear again convinced that every minute, every second, would make a difference. All stoplights looked green to me regardless of the stopped cars, and I swerved in and out of traffic to get to where I needed to be: *with Isabelle.* I could fix what was wrong if I was there. I was her mom.

I parked next to Chad's truck at the Emergency entrance and waited in line inside the front door to have my photo taken for a name badge. There was absolutely no sense of urgency about the pudgy man behind the desk when he told me to "smile" for the camera.

"Seriously!" I snapped and in an instant he understood that I was using the emergency entrance for an actual emergency. He didn't look up at me again while we waited a freakishly long time for the miniature printer to spit out my name tag. I slapped the sticker on my chest, he pressed a button and I pushed open the heavy metal doors to the ICU. A nurse caught up with me immediately and I was escorted to a tiny waiting room with a chair and a couch crammed inside. Chad sat on the edge of the couch, hunched over next to his mom, Karen.

"She's not here yet," Chad said and barely glanced at me.

I wondered if I had gone to the hospital by our house—where Isabelle was originally brought—if I could have gotten into the helicopter and been airlifted with her. Why didn't I think of that? I could have been with her this whole time. Why hadn't Carla called me? I was mere minutes from the hospital. I could have been with her, making everything better.

"How long?" I asked, my leg bouncing in its usual response to stress.

"Twenty minutes or so."

I nodded and watched Chad stare at the floor.

"Have they said anything?" I asked. "The doctors…since you got here?"

He shook his head and looked kind of mad. I knew this man and he wasn't mad at me. It was concern, worry, and fear that gave his face a drawn look. The last thing he needed was twenty questions from me. He had enough questions of his own, I guessed, so I sat back in the chair and exhaled so sharply that a little whistle came from inside me. I poked relentlessly at my cuticles even though Mom had always instructed me not to touch them unless my fingers were softened from a shower or a bath. Normal rules didn't apply to me now. Something terrible was happening. I chipped away at the red nail polish on my thumb. I knew what I had to do. I had to ask for help from God.

Chapter Seven

I was standing in the hallway of the ICU, pressed against a cold brick wall for support, when three paramedics rushed by with a little boy on a stretcher. My eyes followed him, heavyhearted, a flurry of activity around him and tubes splayed over his little body.

"That was her!" Jennie shouted as she rushed around the corner.

I turned so quickly that I lost my balance and nearly fell. *That little boy? That was my little girl?* My throat burned with acidic disbelief, and at the same second I turned to rush toward her, a doctor stepped in front of me and led me back into the family waiting room. He said something about Isabelle being without oxygen, five minutes or so, Carla thought. Isabelle had been down for a nap. Carla checked on her. She wasn't breathing. Carla gave her CPR. The first officer on the scene was able to get her heart started again. She hadn't been breathing for ten, maybe fifteen minutes by that time. Isabelle struggled a little when the paramedics forced a breathing tube down her throat. That was a good sign, he said. They scrambled to get an IV in her arm, and when they couldn't, they stuck it into her leg instead.

"That was smart. That's what I would have done," the doctor said. "Her body was traumatized and might have the ability to recover in a comatose state."

"Might?" I asked. My vision blurred, my cheeks went numb, and I squinted to bring this tall man into focus. I didn't want to miss a movement, a telling sign of her condition.

The doctor swallowed hard and his large Adam's apple sank, then bobbed up again. "I need to assess the situation. I haven't seen her yet, just received reports from the paramedics."

He told us his name but I didn't commit it to memory. I didn't want to know him or know what other children he'd seen or how he would compare them to Isabelle. I only wanted to know that she was going to be okay.

"You can see her in a few minutes," he said, then paused. "I just want to warn you that she might be a little cold to the touch. She went a significant amount of time without oxygen."

My hands raked back and forth through my hair as I paced the hallway with Chad for the next five minutes. I breathed hard. *In through my nose, out through my mouth.* My breathing was the only thing I could control, and even that felt iffy.

When we got clearance to visit Isabelle, my feet were glued to the linoleum floor. I was afraid. Scared stiff to see Isabelle in that condition. But I was her mommy and mommies always made things better. Maybe just hearing my voice or feeling my touch could bring her back safely to us. Chad reached for my hand and I took it, walking half a step behind him into the room. I barely recognized her on the stretcher and the shock doubled me over, but I was able to move quickly to her side. Her skin was cold, but not as cold as I feared it would be. She had a tube in her nose and a gluey substance above her lip. Her leg was already starting to bruise at the point where the IV was inserted. She was scarred and damaged and I couldn't do a damn thing about it.

The doctor explained the monitors to us. Her heartbeat was much lower than he wanted to see it after a "situation" like hers: 64 beats per minute and he wanted to see it near 140. I knew very little about medical terms or how the body's systems and organs worked together. "If her heart's beating, doesn't that mean she can breathe on her own?"

"No," the doctor said. "The machine is doing the breathing for her. If we take that out—" he pointed to the tube, "—we don't know if she'd be able to breathe on her own."

He explained that the next 24 hours would be critical and her improvement, or lack thereof, would determine her fate. Several nurses, doctors, and specialists hustled into the room, and Chad and I were asked to sit in the waiting room while they moved Isabelle from the paramedic's stretcher to the bed in Room No. 2.

I sat next to Chad, silent, and listened in disbelief as he explained the situation to his dad who'd just arrived. Halfway through the summary, a lady in her mid-forties popped her head into the room.

"I'm the hospital chaplain," she said. "I'm here if anyone needs to talk."

At first I couldn't grasp what a chaplain was, then the word "God" flashed in front of my eyes, causing white-hot anger to consume me. I held up my hand.

"We're fine," I said, not looking at her, and, as Chad finished giving his dad details, I cursed God: *How could you do this to us? How could you put me through what I went through when Isabelle was first born, let me start to feel better, let us bond, get into a routine, then drop this bomb on us? You better hope that she pulls through this or else...*

When Chad and his family went out into the hallway, I called Mom's work, but they said she'd left for the day. When I called her at home our conversation was brief. I told her what I'd learned from the doctor and she told me she had been on the Internet and would be on a plane from Florida by tomorrow. She said she'd called my sister and that Kim was looking at flights, too.

This is a full-blown crisis, I thought as I sat alone in the family waiting room, which seemed to have taken on an eerie green glow. Chad had taken a walk with his mom and I wasn't sure what to do with myself. I tried to cry, but no tears came. Shock didn't leave room for tears—only distorted vision and labored breathing. I chipped a little more at the red nail polish, put my hands together, tentatively at first, then clasped them so hard my fingertips bore into my knuckles. I closed my eyes and exhaled hard. What did I have to lose?

"Please God, please God, please," I hissed over and over. That's all I could say and I hoped he knew what I was praying for. Details didn't seem necessary, but I whispered Isabelle's name at the end just to be sure.

* * *

It was the longest afternoon/evening of my life, and my cell phone rang repeatedly with calls from Carla. I sent her straight to voicemail, then finally asked Jennie to be in charge of calling her with periodic updates.

"I bet she feels so bad," Jennie said.

"Don't we all?" I snapped, then felt mean when Jennie recoiled. I knew she wasn't implying that we weren't all suffering or that Carla might feel worse than Chad or me, but I didn't want sympathy lost on anyone else. All energy needed to be focused on Isabelle.

Finally I said, "I do wonder if I would have known what to do if this had happened at our house." That diffused the situation a little and Jennie sat down next to me. I continued. "Maybe that's why she went to day care today. A Monday. She doesn't normally go to day care on Mondays."

Later, Jennie relayed her conversation with Carla to me. "Carla and her husband were just getting ready to go to their church when I called."

"Why?" I asked.

"To pray for Isabelle," Jennie said. "I told her you don't blame her. That you were thankful Isabelle was at her house when it happened."

Fury blazed in my cheeks and spread to my ears, and to keep me from snapping at my well-meaning sister-in-law, I left the room. I never said I didn't blame Carla. I never said I was glad Isabelle was at day care. I was just talking. Thinking out loud. I found Chad and went on a rant.

"Maybe I do blame Carla," I said. "I don't even know what happened. Maybe it was her fault."

Whether or not *it* was her fault depended on what *it* turned out to be: a close brush with death or the loss of my daughter. If Isabelle was okay, I imagined I could forgive just about anything. If not, I needed someone to blame.

Chad looked exhausted and reminded me that when Isabelle took naps at home we rarely checked on her. Our 1950s wood floors were very creaky and if we peeked into her room, we risked cutting her nap short.

"I know, I know," I said. "I just don't know what to do with myself."

I needed to be with Isabelle, and I was on my way to her room when a lady from social services and a police department detective appeared to question Chad and me individually. They were polite, but I still felt like I was on trial when they asked question after question during an interrogation process that stretched over half an hour. Why did I bring Isabelle to day care that day when I normally had her home with me on Mondays? Did Chad have any anger issues? Did I consider myself a good mother? Had Isabelle spent a significant amount of time with anyone else over the last week?

Finally the female detective flipped her notebook closed and said, "Well, I think that's it. You seem to be doing very well. Holding together well."

I looked up. "I'm not."

She looked away. "It might help you to know that we spoke to Carla and it really seemed that she did everything she could to help Isabelle."

I didn't want to talk about Carla. I stood up and opened the family waiting room door. "Do you need to talk to Chad now?"

She nodded and I directed her to my husband. She quickly separated us so we couldn't compare notes.

Over the next two hours, every member of Chad's immediate family came to visit our little girl, a tiny baby on a giant table wearing only a diaper. Tubes criss-crossed this way and that and a miniature pulse-oximetry sensor was clipped to her big toe to measure her oxygen saturation levels. A heat lamp overhead kept her warm, and the nurses were constantly turning it on and off to maintain just the right temperature. It crushed me to see Chad's dad's expression when he saw his granddaughter. Dale gave a quick glance, a squeeze of her little hand, and left the room. I saw the sheer devastation on his face and wanted to comfort him somehow. I knew he didn't want to cry in front of us, so I cried for him.

Isabelle's heartbeat had increased to a level that Nurse Chris said was within the range we wanted to see, but when the doctor arrived to have a final look at her before he went home for the evening, he didn't seem impressed.

"I'd like to see some movement," he said. "Fingers twitching, eyes opening."

He pulled up her lids and shined a flashlight in her eyes. I couldn't look. And when he left I was pissed at him for not saying more. Maybe I wanted him to comfort us. He was a doctor, though, and I sensed he'd seen situations like this before. It scared me that he might already know Isabelle's fate, and it scared me even more that I might know it, too.

Around 11 p.m. I believed God actually heard me. Chad, his mom, his sisters, and I encircled Isabelle's bed and we each jumped when her arm twitched, then a finger, then a little movement of her head. The breathing monitor showed spots of gray, which Nurse Chris said indicated times when the monitor thought she was breathing on her own. It wasn't always exact, though, he warned us.

Isabelle's eyes flickered open now and then, and Chad stroked her head.

"There's my baby girl," he whispered. "Let Daddy see those big, brown eyes."

I didn't try to hide my excitement and even broke down with happy tears as I imagined us being one of those lucky families that narrowly escaped tragedy. The excitement continued in the room for about an hour, then a dreadful feeling crept over me. I tried to ignore it and partake in the celebration, but I knew something. Something awful.

"Is she waking up?" I finally asked Nurse Chris. "Her movements seem too rhythmic …almost like—"

Nurse Chris scooted closer on his wheeled stool and gave Isabelle his full attention. I'd noticed him watching us several times in the last hour, watching Isabelle, but he never commented on her status.

"She's most likely having seizures," he said lightly, then lifted her eyelid and shined a light into her eye.

I blinked and looked away.

"I'd like to see her respond to the light, but she's not," Nurse Chris said.

Maya Angelou once claimed that hope and fear could not occupy the same space. "Pick one to stay," she'd written. But both hope and fear existed in me at that moment, fighting for a front row spot and beating me up in the process.

I tried to give "seizures" a positive spin. Seizures equaled brain activity, didn't they? I gently laid my upper body over Isabelle's, trying to hug her around the tubes and sensors, but the shaking only grew in intensity. Midnight came and went, and I stood at the end of her bed, slightly bent over as fatigue engulfed me. Jennie suggested I go lay down for a little bit in one of the sleeping rooms and, although I didn't want to leave Isabelle's side, I felt my mind starting to race as the stress of the day settled on my shoulders. Jennie had made the trip to our house and picked up some things for us, and at my request, she'd brought my Ambien and my journal to the hospital. If there was ever a time I'd have trouble sleeping, I knew this would be the night.

Chad reminded me that the doctor, before he left for the night, had also insisted that we get some sleep.

"Sometimes parents begin to hallucinate when they're overly tired," he'd said. "They might imagine their baby waking up or moving when those things aren't really happening."

I gave in. One of the nurses gave us a key to Sleeping Room 1925. Parents typically had to sign up each afternoon to have the room reserved for that evening, but she said we could have it for as many days as we needed it.

"That's not a good sign," I said to Chad, and we leaned heavily on each other as we made our way to the room.

When I woke at 6 a.m., I took a shower and brushed my teeth. At the height of my postpartum depression, my counselor had told me that I would be no good to Isabelle if I didn't take care of myself. So I forced a fruit smoothie down my throat before I walked the long hallway to her room. There was a new nurse at the door and Chad was already by Isabelle's bedside. His stare was blank when I entered, and with Isabelle's first twitch I knew the seizures hadn't stopped.

"Let's go for a walk," Chad said.

We walked down the hallway and finally settled into the family waiting room.

"What are we going to do?" I sobbed. "What are we going to do if she doesn't make it?"

I was sprawled awkwardly on the couch and Chad kneeled on the floor, his hands wrapped around mine.

"We have family," he said, squeezing me. "We'll get through this."

I shook my head violently. "I can't be without her. I can't!"

"Amy," he said with a little force. He took my face in his hands. "We'll get through this."

I wanted to believe him. God, how I wanted to believe him, but it just wasn't possible. If Isabelle didn't make it, I'd be done.

Chad's mom and sister, Andre, arrived a short time later and Chad left the room to update them on Isabelle's condition. I called Mom, who was scheduled to arrive at 4 p.m. I looked at the clock: 7:30 a.m. Four o'clock seemed like a world away, but if I could make it to 4 p.m., I felt like I might be okay. My dad and sister had also booked flights from Florida and were scheduled to arrive that night at 10 p.m.

Real estate might not have been my career of choice, but I knew there was a strong support system of 200-plus agents and staff members. They rallied together when one of their own faced a difficult situation and I really needed their strength. Pete, my coworker from the real estate office, was the first one to use the dreaded acronym when I called him with the news that we were at Children's Hospital.

"So, do they think it's SIDS?" Pete asked and I shuddered.

"I don't know," I said and gave him the rundown of what I did know. Pete told me about his sister-in-law who lost a baby several years ago, and when he said the boy had stopped breathing at day care my ears perked up and my heart plummeted.

"Is she okay? I mean, how do you go on after something like that?" I asked.

Pete didn't go into details, and I sensed he didn't know how to respond to me, not knowing if Isabelle would make it or not. His question, "Do they think it's SIDS?" lingered in my mind later when the doctor arrived to check on Isabelle. As far as I was concerned it couldn't be Sudden Infant Death Syndrome. Isabelle was still alive.

Jennie called Pastor Tom from Cross of Peace Church where Isabelle was baptized. When he arrived, I felt both comfort and a twinge of anger. Pastor Tom was the closest link I had to God, but God had a lot of explaining to do.

"What is the point of praying?" I asked him as he stood next to me by Isabelle's bed.

Pastor Tom looked at me. Expressionless.

"I mean, what good is it to pray if this is 'part of God's plan'?" I asked, making air quotes above my head. "What's the point if he's already decided what will happen to her?"

Pastor Tom put his hand on my shoulder. I felt the heat instantly, a calming warmth.

"I don't believe that God pulls strings," he said simply.

I looked to him, confused. "What does that mean?"

There were tears in his eyes. "I believe God is crying for Isabelle right now, just as we are."

I didn't believe it. Here was this all-knowing, all-powerful God who gave Moses the power to part the Red Sea and had Jesus rise from the dead, but he couldn't help Isabelle? And crying with us? I doubted that. But I wanted to believe what Pastor Tom had to say because I believed in him. I couldn't clear my foggy mind enough to comprehend any of what he said, but I did wonder how miracles factored into all of this. God always got the credit for those. How did he decide if a situation was miracle worthy? Shouldn't he be blamed for the non-miracles, too, or times like this when it seemed he'd completely dropped the ball?

I went off on my own again into the privacy of the small family waiting room. "God!" I said out loud to make sure he heard me. I was perched on the edge of the couch with my hands squeezed so hard together that my knuckles turned white. "You have to help me. You have to save my little girl. Please, pull Isabelle through this." I bit down hard on my lower lip and tasted the metallic tang of blood.

"If…if you save her, God, I'm yours forever. Your biggest fan. But if you take her from me, you and me, we are done. I will never speak your name again."

* * *

Jennie picked up Mom at the airport and she rushed into Isabelle's room at 4:30 p.m., her suitcase dropped somewhere between the ICU entrance and Room No. 2. Tears gushed from her eyes and the color drained from her face when she saw her granddaughter. The sight of my mother's heartache made me breakdown. Part of me had hoped Mom would saunter into the room, wave her hand and say, "She looks fine. She'll be up and moving in no time," but Mom wasn't a doctor and that was an unfair expectation of her. Her tears confirmed the worst for me, and inside my weary body, Hope stepped solemnly out of the ring, and Fear raised its arms in victory.

Chapter Eight

I needed to take a break from standing over Isabelle's bed and that need to step away from my daughter stirred up a thick batch of guilt inside of me. Guilt was a close friend of Fear's and he'd become an unwanted next-door neighbor to me. I was getting used to him lounging around on his front porch, smelly cigar in one hand and a beer in the other, watching my every move, waiting for the chance to waggle his finger at me and say, *Uh, uh, uh, a good mother wouldn't do that.*

I walked the hospital hallways in search of some sign of change that might have occurred in the last hour, but the rooms still housed the same patients, the nurses still poured over their charts, and a doctor buzzed through every now and then wearing the same hurried expression. I had secretly hoped during my ten, sometimes fifteen, minute breaks that I would round the corner of the ICU to Room No. 2 and there would be a flurry of activity around Isabelle's bed. Nurses would claim a miracle as they touched her tiny body, doctors with stethoscopes would shake their heads in blissful bewilderment, and someone would cheer, *The baby is awake! And there appears to be no signs of brain damage.*

Word had spread quickly about Isabelle, and I received dozens of e-mails on my Blackberry from my inner and outer circles. My two best friends, Jen and Marti, knew what a private person I was and they text messaged me every couple of hours for updates. I didn't have much to tell them, but I appreciated that they knew me well enough to know not to call. And they were respectful of the fact that I had asked security not to allow visitors into the ICU other than family members. The security request was a last minute grasp for control of something, anything. But somehow they managed to screw that up. Maybe it was an oversight. Maybe it was a mistake. Later I would wonder if the visitor that came that day was sent to me as something more.

I made my way to the large family waiting area where there was a television, refrigerator, couches, chairs, and piles of outdated magazines. I had just found a spot in the corner, leaned up against a cream-colored wall, when Hilary, a woman I barely knew from the real estate office, entered through the double doors. She carried a giant wicker basket filled with crackers, cookies, and bottles of water. As Hilary approached, I felt a "POP!" and I knew that the protective bubble I'd spent the morning surrounding myself with was gone. So much for the imaginary shield that had allowed me for the last two days to totter along, partially absent, not fully seeing or comprehending the tragedy unfolding before me.

"Hi Amy," she said, her voice soft but, thankfully, not pitying. She set the basket by my side. Hilary was a pretty girl with a short blonde bob, probably in her early thirties like me, and always wearing the most perfectly applied lipstick of anyone I knew. At that moment it annoyed me that she wore lipstick when I hadn't even bothered to brush my hair in two days. Hilary was an acquaintance with whom I'd only exchanged a handful of words during the past two years. She worked in the title department, and every now and then when I had a closing, she was the facilitator.

I became aware of words coming from her: "…and I don't know what to do in this situation. I'm afraid nothing I say will be of much comfort," Hilary's lips said to me, "but I'd like to pray with you. That's all I know to do right now."

Seriously? My mind snapped to attention. *Pray?* I looked into her green eyes and felt shock, embarrassment, anger, and a sense of surrealism rumble through me, the beginnings of an earthquake. Would this be a good time to tell her I despised God? I wanted to suggest that she pray to him by herself. He might listen to her. But the Minnesota Nice got the best of me and I rose to my feet, reluctantly taking her little hand. I wasn't so upset that she'd somehow weaseled her way past security or that she'd brought the basket of treats. I was more peeved that she'd brought *Him* with her. As far as I was concerned, God had no place in the hospital or anywhere in my life again.

Chad materialized by my side and formed a circle with Hilary and me. My hands were sweaty as he took one palm and Hilary squeezed the other. I glanced up to see Chad's head bowed slightly, so I bowed mine too. Hilary spoke loudly like she didn't care about anyone else in the room but the people she held hands with, and Isabelle, a baby she'd never even met. She said things like "Dear God," "Almighty Jesus," and "Precious Lord" with such emphasis and passion that I felt tremors roll through me.

I stared at the white, speckled linoleum floor tiles and watched as each tear hit the ground—from my eyes, from Chad's eyes, and from Hilary's eyes. Hilary prayed that God would make the doctors "especially keen" the next day when Isabelle was scheduled to have her MRI to determine the extent of her brain injuries. Hilary was a small girl with a sweet personality and an even sweeter smile, but there was nothing particularly soft-spoken about her prayer style. No, she was resolute and determined, like she really believed in this higher power, and when she practically shouted, "Lord, we know that in our weakness God's strength is made perfect," the words shook my very foundation, rattling my windows and banging my doors.

My eyes, which had closed sometime during her prayer, flickered open, and aftershocks rolled through my arms and legs as I repeated that sentence in my head: "In our weakness God's strength is made perfect?" *Really. Is it really? And how?* I tried to develop a mental picture of what *our weakness* and *God's strength* looked like, but images failed me. I felt it, though. I felt my weakness, and as my hand tightened around Hilary's, I felt the intensity of God's strength radiate through to the epicenter of my body. I recognized the feeling from the day in the Petco parking lot, when I had planned to end my life.

* * *

An hour later I sat alone in our sleeping room trying to make sense of the last two days and how I'd spent them pleasantly pissed off at God. He'd sent a chaplain and Pastor Tom and even Hilary to do his dirty work. What I still didn't understand was why he hadn't intercepted the whole tragedy by being with Isabelle at day care. More than that, I didn't understand why Hilary's words, which I assumed came from the Bible, seemingly blasted apart my carefully constructed sanctimonious walls and left me with this gaping hole, exposed. And with all of that obliteration, I felt a calm that I couldn't place.

I hadn't heard the rest of what Hilary had said, but I knew she said it with gusto, and when she finished with "Amen," I said "Amen" too.

But I was beside myself. Something had happened inside of me and I felt too paralyzed by the prayer to question it. Hilary left as quietly as she'd come, but her words continued to ring loud in my ears, making it hard to hear anything else.

* * *

Chad and I logged a lot of miles around Children's Hospital and the neighboring Abbott-Northwestern Hospital that evening, despite the sweltering July temperatures. The doctor shared again that he "wasn't impressed" with Isabelle's progress, and he said we would look for more information from the MRI that would be done the next morning. In the meantime all we could do was wait. Her seizures had subsided, most likely due to the medication that the nurses continually pumped into her little body, but there was still no sign of movement. The breathing monitor showed little flashes of gray, but less than before.

At 9 p.m., Chad finally talked me into going to bed. He wanted us to get some sleep so we could be up early in the morning for the MRI. I popped a sleeping pill and crash-landed into dreamland. My dad and sister arrived at 11 p.m. and I vaguely remember waking to greet them as they deposited their suitcases in the room.

I was awake again at 3 a.m. and paced the hallways until I collapsed around 6 a.m. into a reclining chair that someone had placed outside of Isabelle's room. Moments later Dad found me and slid onto the armrest. I hugged him tight.

"Thanks for coming," I said as the tears pooled.

Dad didn't speak, just rubbed my arm. I was especially grateful that he came, since he had an aversion to airplanes and hospitals. My grandma and grandpa, his parents, had died a year-and-a-half before within one month of each other and the whole idea of illness gave him panic attacks. Dad and I weren't close like Mom and I were; our relationship was different. We didn't have in-depth conversations and I didn't share my deepest dreams and desires with him, but I knew I could count on him like the grass could count on rain. And in that moment while he stroked my arm, I felt thankful to have him next to me. We talked about God a little. I told him about Hilary's prayer and I asked him if he ever prayed.

"Sometimes," he said, but didn't elaborate.

I wished at that moment I had put forth a little more effort in confirmation class. Maybe I would have learned the secret password to unlock the window to God's world so that I could ensure my Isabelle prayers were being heard.

"I've been praying," I said as if it were a confession.

"So have I," he said, and I heard his breath catch. He held himself back from crying. I could tell. Dad hardly ever cried, but he had very expressive eyes. He rarely had the words to share his feelings, so he rarely shared, but I could almost always read his emotions in his gray-blue eyes. So when I asked him if he believed the cliché that "everything happens for a reason," I looked to his eyes, not his mouth for the answer. The tears formed but they didn't spill over. He shook his head gently.

"I don't know, Aim. I don't know," he said, and I appreciated his honesty. I guessed that everything he thought he knew about life had gone right down the drain in the last couple of days.

"I do know, though, that this is the hardest thing you'll ever have to go through in your life," he said and captured me in a hug.

A nurse interrupted us to say the MRI was pushed back to 4 p.m. to accommodate some fancy neurologist from another hospital, and that the doctor had also ordered electrode monitoring to measure Isabelle's brain activity. The electrode procedure could be done in the hospital room; whereas the MRI would be done in a room at the other end of the building.

By 9 a.m., all of our family members were back at the hospital. I set up post in Isabelle's room with my journal and a fruit smoothie—the only nourishment I'd been able to force down in two days. Chad passed by once with his mom and I smiled weakly at him. Our interactions were interesting and it seemed that in the worst moments when my head slipped just below the surface, Chad had the strength to pull me back up. I hoped I could do the same for him.

A doctor shuffled into Isabelle's room with an elaborate system on wheels and proceeded to press a variety of clear plastic electrodes to my baby's body. The process made the back of my tongue cramp like it did just before I threw up. I couldn't watch the screen, but Mom did, and when the procedure was done she said she saw lines going up and down.

"I don't know what that means," she said as she rubbed my shoulders, "but it seems like it'd be a good thing. Like maybe the lines were brain activity."

There was cheering in my head. Hope reentered the ring, weak but ready for battle, and with that surge of emotion, fatigue engulfed me again. I started to cry. Through my tears, I watched as my sister, Kim, read book after book to Isabelle with all of the excitement and voice changes that a person would use to entertain a fully coherent infant. I always knew I loved my sister because, well, I was legally obligated to love her. But as I watched her animated facial expressions I felt a new depth of love for her, almost like she was an extension of me. I couldn't read to Isabelle because the tears and sobs made my body limp and my voice hoarse, but Kim could read to her and that felt like the next best thing.

An hour later Mom caught me yawning and rubbing my face. "You need to go lay down right now and try to get more sleep before the MRI," Mom said and I nodded. Her bossiness was simply her way of looking out for my best interests. I recognized that and I was thankful for it.

Kim folded closed the last of the picture books in her pile and walked me to the sleeping room. I popped another sleeping pill and lay down on the bed. I had a good fifteen-to-twenty minutes before my racing mind slowed and I'd be subdued into sleep. Kim sat on the floor next to the bed and I found an extraordinary level of comfort in her presence. My sister was six years younger than me, and our dealings with each other hadn't always been pleasant. We fought over clothes in our younger years, and I always enjoyed rummaging in her closet because she was the clotheshorse. My need to control situations always irked her and we often got into arguments that started with her urging me to "settle down," which fueled my fire even more. Yet, we'd become committed to being more than family members. We truly were sisters, and as each year passed our age gap seemed to grow smaller and smaller.

"You'll do something with this," Kim said as she picked through the miscellaneous items in her purse. "Whatever the outcome, you'll do something with this."

I looked at her purse and thought about making a sarcastic comment about *doing something* with her Coach satchel, but I couldn't even make a joke. Instead I lay there silently. My mind, still coherent, struggled with her comment: *Do what? What will I do? Nothing. Because there is nothing left for me if Isabelle isn't here.*

"Joey and I talked about how, no matter what happens, you'll do something with this experience," Kim continued, relaying her earlier phone conversation with her boyfriend. "Joey said, 'Knowing your sister, she'll go on a crusade or do something big with all of this.'"

I didn't argue. I was known for my *mission possible* mentality when I was particularly passionate about something. But as far as a *crusade* went, there was no chance my life could go on without Isabelle.

My eyelids became heavier, only opening halfway after each blink. I didn't say anything for a while—and that was the beauty of being with my sister. I didn't have to fill the silence and she didn't talk until her distant voice told me she was going to get something to eat and I should get some sleep.

* * *

Late that afternoon, a cluster of doctors shifted Isabelle carefully onto a stretcher to take her to the other side of the building for her MRI. We weren't allowed to follow. Moments later, a chubby male nurse passed by and commented, "Wow, she looks swollen."

I lost it. "Get out of here!" I shouted, charging him like a raging ram whose offspring was threatened. "You don't say that. Why would you say that? What's the matter with you?"

His face crumpled and deep creases lined his forehead. I didn't give him a chance to defend himself, just angrily waved him away as I watched Isabelle wheeled down the hallway away from me.

"Have you gotten any sleep?" the doctor asked me as he took a piece of paper from the nurse.

I nodded. "I have sleeping pills."

He looked at me with judgment. "You know it's better if you can sleep without those."

I felt my ears pull back as my mouth dropped open. "Seriously?" I muttered as he turned and left the room.

When Nurse Chris arrived for his evening shift I told him first about the stupid nurse's comment, then about the doctor's recommendation that I not take sleeping pills.

"Seriously?" he said, shaking his head. "What a jerk."

"I know," I said, finally feeling like someone was on my side. I loved Nurse Chris. I knew nothing about him, really, but I loved how gentle he was when he looked into Isabelle's eyes or moved her ever-so-slightly when it appeared she might be in an uncomfortable position. He knew and I knew that she probably couldn't feel discomfort, but I assumed he did it more for me than for her. That made me love him. And I loved his shoes. His tennis shoes were sparkling clean and it seemed he wore a different pair each time I saw him. White with a blue Nike swoosh. Gray with a red Reebok symbol. If there was one thing I knew for sure in that uncertain time, it was that Nurse Chris was in the right profession.

Nurse Chris and I talked about how long he'd been in his position, the light blue awareness bracelet he wore on his wrist for one of his patients who was fighting cancer, and how he found the strength to work in the ICU. We talked about everything except Isabelle, and when Chad rushed into the room, wondering if Isabelle was back from her MRI, I broke down. Chad tried to comfort me, but he started crying, too.

"Come on guys," Nurse Chris said with sincere sympathy as he scooted closer on his swivel stool. "Don't give up hope. I've seen amazing things come out of this hospital."

I believed him. I believed he'd seen amazing things, but there were some things you just knew. And I was afraid I just knew.

By midnight, each member of our family had gone home for the night or had retreated to one of the sleeping rooms. I stayed in Isabelle's room. I didn't want her to be alone even though there was a nurse in the room at all times. While I was there, two of the night nurses gave her a sponge bath and tied a pink ribbon around her little Izzy Hawk hairdo. Chad and I often joked that there was no taming her baby Mohawk, even when Mom licked her hand and tried to plaster the hairs down before Isabelle's baptism picture.

The nurse on duty, who gave Nurse Chris a break, offered me baby lotion to rub on Isabelle and I carefully adjusted cords so I could caress her little body. She wore pink socks and I slipped them off so I could rub her tiny toes. With each swipe of my fingernail along the arch of her foot, I watched her face, then I tickled just under her ribs and poked under her arm pits—her tickle buttons. But there was no movement. I put Vaseline on her partially parted lips, watching her tongue. The doctor had said that he wanted to see Isabelle's tongue move and resist the tube that was down her throat. That would have been a good sign to him. Her tongue didn't move, though, so I leaned close to Isabelle's face.

"Please wake up, baby girl," I whispered. "Or give my finger a little squeeze so I know you can hear me."

She twitched a few times but the nurse said she was most likely having muscle spasms from her body being sedentary for so long. I asked the nurse if I could turn the heat lamp on and she nodded. Then I slipped into the reclining chair in the corner and watched the monitors. There were brief blips of gray.

"That's probably just from the tube that helps her breathe," the nurse said, watching me.

I wished they'd get their stories straight. Were the gray spots a good sign or not? I wasn't about to argue with her. I didn't have the energy. I wrapped a blanket around myself and tried to shove Saltine crackers between my lips.

The nurse on duty tried to talk to me, but I wasn't a very good conversationalist. I took out my notebook and jotted down words and phrases to describe my feelings. "Tragedy." "Traumatized." "Insurmountable loss." When I flipped to the second page I became instantly aware of what I was doing and it made my heart skip with the realization. I covered my mouth to stop the sobs. I'd caught myself making notes for the tragic book I would write about losing my four-month-old daughter and how it caused me to spiral into insanity. I ripped the page from the notebook and forced myself to journal instead.

Wednesday, July 25—*The Witching Hours*

Nurse Chris called me a caretaker tonight and reminded me that I also have to take care of myself. Caretaker. Maybe that's an appropriate term for me on a good day, but I'm pretty sure caretaker would not be the best word to describe me tonight.

I sent Dad and Kim to stay at my house, to shower and to get a good night's sleep. I sent Mom to the sleeping room and set Chad up in an empty room next to Isabelle's where he promptly fell asleep on one of the hospital beds. How is it that my husband can sleep anywhere?

I'm sitting with Isabelle now. I can only stare at her and hold her tiny hand and rub her soft skin for so long before I become overwhelmed. I'm teetering on the edge of hope and…something else. I have hope that the MRI will show something positive, that the doctor will look at it with surprise, scratch his chin and say, "Now that's interesting. I've never seen that before, but it sure looks like a good sign." And the miracle will begin.

However, I'm afraid I'm already starting to grieve her loss. I want to believe my little baby is still in that lifeless body, but I just don't know.

So, as far as being a caretaker, I'm actually thinking more about myself tonight than everyone else. When I sent them all away, to bed, I had a moment of strength and I wanted everyone to sleep, rejuvenate, and gain some of their own endurance back. Tomorrow they will become my caretakers.

There was no change in Isabelle's condition overnight and around noon the next day, the fancy neurologist from another hospital arrived in Isabelle's room where most of our family waited.

"The electrode tests show a possibility that Isabelle might be able to breathe on her own," he said, making direct eye contact with me, "but probably not."

I winced and he looked away.

"She most likely wouldn't be able to speak or show emotion. She wouldn't walk or have arm movements."

I looked at my baby girl, kept alive by machines and medicine. This really wasn't happening, was it? To me? I'd prayed like a madwoman the last two days and Jen told me that her church—a mega establishment with a thousand-some members—had started a prayer chain. There had to be someone in that bunch with a solid connection. Even Pastor Tom was at the hospital every day.

The neurologist didn't have any more to say, and when he left, I exited the room as calmly as possible, hoping that no one would follow me. I slipped into the small family waiting room where I held tight to the beginning of my downward spiral. I fell to my knees on the couch, then punched the floral pattern. Again and again and again. Fists throbbing. Punch. Punch. Punch. No relief. Hiss. Punch. Punch. I sobbed. I couldn't breathe.

What the hell am I going to do with myself? my mind screamed. I wanted out of this life, out of this place. I smashed my face into the couch and screamed as hard as I could, feeling hot air push through the fabric. I squeezed my hands into fists with so much force that my thumbs cracked. I couldn't yell into the couch loud enough or hit the furniture hard enough to bring relief. I exhausted myself within minutes, but I had a little kick left in me. I rolled to a hunched-over sitting position and clapped my hands together hard.

"Fine!" I hissed through clenched teeth. "You've got one more chance!"

I pressed my eyes closed tight and tried to strike a deal with God. If he would let me keep Isabelle, I told him, I would devote my entire life to teaching people about SIDS. Or, if Isabelle had to be in a wheelchair with a brain injury, I would lead the quest for funding to help others with brain injuries.

"I'll become the spokesperson for God's sake! Whatever you want me to do!" I fell onto my back on the couch and slapped my hands over my face.

Just then Mom busted through the door. "Oh, my gosh!," she said, breathing hard. "There you are. You're dad's going crazy. He thought you ran off. He thought you might—"

I sat up.

"I'll be right back," she said and held her hand out to me. "Stay here. I've got to find him before he makes himself nuts looking for you."

The door shut and it dawned on me. My family was afraid I would kill myself. Suicide hadn't even occurred to me. And why? Why hadn't it occurred to me? This was the kind of situation during which thoughts of suicide might actually be expected, accepted even, and instead I imagined my future in a Ward for Whackos.

I dropped my head into my hands. "Because people who kill themselves don't go to Heaven!" I spat, hating God more than ever. He wouldn't even give me an out.

Mom and Dad entered the room, Dad with relief to see me sitting on the couch. My throat closed up as they rushed to me and I sobbed into their shoulders while they knelt on the floor.

"What am I going to do?" I bellowed and I felt their bodies shake in response. They let me cry and gasp for air for several minutes before Dad sat back.

"You have to wait for that MRI," he said. "This was just one doctor's opinion. Don't give up yet."

I looked to him with the expectancy of a little girl, hoping that the lessons he'd learned in his sixty years had given him the kind of wisdom I didn't yet possess. Hope was a strong little bugger, hanging onto that rope with all her might as Fear tried repeatedly to kick her out of the game. The electrode test results were bleak, but I did what Dad said. I waited for the MRI results.

Chapter Nine

The nurse on duty brought a two-person padded bench into the room and rearranged Isabelle's wires, so that each of our family members could hold her. I knew what all of it meant and it took everything I had left in me, which wasn't much, to stand in the doorway and watch. My sister must have sensed my uneasiness, because she linked her arm with mine and walked me upstairs to the chapel. She was several inches shorter than me but comforted me like a king-size blanket when she slipped her arm around my waist.

The chapel was a small room with traditional stained-glass windows flanking the heavy wooden door. Kim led me to kneel on a bench in the front of the room near a large cross and a wooden table with a colorful palette of candles flickering their greeting.

"We're going to pray now," she said matter-of-factly, then folded her hands together.

I noticed her bit-to-the-nubbin fingernails and checked my own. There were only a few splotches of red paint remaining. Kim cleared her throat and proceeded to talk to God in a normal, everyday voice. Her method was so different from the fervor of Hilary's prayer, but then again Kim was a very different girl from Hilary. Kim was soft and sweet, too, when she wanted to be, but she also possessed a hard edge that kept outsiders from getting too close, from seeing too much, until she was good and ready. And I suspected it was that hard edge that she relied on now, because I hadn't seen her cry once since she'd arrived.

Yet, my twenty-five-year-old sister opened up completely in that chapel, begging God to help me and to give me strength. She didn't ask him specifically to fix Isabelle, but she sure implied it, and I wondered if she'd done this praying thing before. She was pretty good at it. She asked me if I wanted to say anything and I shook my head. We sat for a minute in silence, then she got up and led me back to Isabelle's room. When we arrived, I half hoped the nurse would tell me there'd been a change in Isabelle's condition or that she was finally waking up. Wasn't that what the power of prayer meant? I prayed; you prayed; we all prayed, and God made a miracle happen. *Bippity-boppity-boo.* There wasn't a change, though, and I took my turn snuggling my baby girl on the two-person bench, wishing I hadn't brought her to day care Monday morning. Wishing I'd spent the morning holding her and playing in the grass like I'd wanted.

A few minutes later the doctor arrived and asked to meet privately with me, Chad, and our parents in the family waiting room. Chad and I sat on the couch, the same couch I had pounded the crap out of an hour before. The doctor knelt on one knee in front of the closed door. Our family had occupied all of the chairs. He told us about the MRI and why MRIs were used to determine the extent of brain damage.

"So, in reviewing the MRI, I believe that if Isabelle were to come out of this coma and were able to breathe again on her own, she would be in a permanent vegetative state."

I fixed my eyes on him, hard, not wanting to move or feel the weight of his words. I wouldn't let his words in. I wouldn't allow them entry. But then I felt the spindly-weak nerves all over my body rise to attention and begin shaking. And the muscles in my neck tensed up, causing my head to move back and forth.

No.

The doctor explained that the MRI "was gray all over," which meant there was damage to Isabelle's entire brain. Sometimes, he said, if the damage is centralized in one area of the brain, other areas can compensate as the child grows.

"But, like I said, the damage isn't centralized," he said.

Chad looked up, his eyes pleading for a different analysis. "But is there a chance? I mean could she be in a wheelchair? I'd love to push her around in a wheelchair."

My breath caught in my throat and I felt his pain piled on top of mine, and for the first time that I'd noticed, the doctor flinched and a muscle ticked at the side of his jaw.

"That's…," he cleared his throat, swallowed, and I fixated on his large Adam's apple as it bobbed up then dropped down, "…that's not going to be an option."

He did offer us the option of a second opinion from a doctor of our choosing and named some of the neighboring hospitals. Then he left the room so we could process the last piece of news we'd been waiting for. And in that moment, Hope officially bowed her head, slid under the ropes of the boxing ring and, without words, declared her defeat.

"You don't have to decide anything right this minute," someone said to our bowed heads, but Chad asked that our families give us time alone.

When it was just us, Chad and I turned to each other and locked hands. I said I couldn't believe this was happening to us. He said he was thankful the doctor's analysis was so cut and dry. He trusted this doctor and I did too, despite the man's nearly unflappable air.

"I knew Monday she wasn't going to make it," Chad said. "I saw the face of Jesus in that picture."

He pointed to the flower picture on the family waiting room wall and tried to show me Jesus' face. I couldn't see it.

Our family waited just outside of Isabelle's room when Chad and I emerged. There were whispers as each person was told what would happen next. I prepared myself for the shock and loathing for what we were about to do, but those looks never appeared. Not one of them questioned our decision or looked upon us with judgment. My parents each put a hand on my shoulders and Chad's mom wrapped her arms around her son. My sister slid in next to me, took my hand and squeezed. No, there was no judgment there, only comfort, loyalty, and protection. I finally felt what I knew Chad had felt all along. My body became engulfed by the warmth of a large family and I let their safety net slip below me, interwoven with the strongest material known to man: unconditional love. I let them be my caretakers.

* * *

Pastor Tom was at the hospital that day, offering comfort and prayers to our family. Chad's mom called more people to come to the hospital, and Chad's best friend Joe and his girlfriend Leslie arrived. I wondered if I should ask Jen and Marti to come, but part of me was already overwhelmed by the number of people there. The irrational part of me felt like they were gawking at my little girl, but the sane part of me—small, but still there—knew they'd come purely in support.

While we waited for the last couple of people to arrive, Chad and I took refuge again in the small family waiting room. We talked about our decision, reassuring ourselves that it was the right thing to do. The best thing to do. Really, the only thing we could do.

"I don't think I can do this," I wheezed, my nose stuffy and my throat raw from crying. "How can we let her go?"

Chad pulled me to him and I let his strong arms envelope my body. He seemed so steadfast in that moment, so together, and his confidence that we were making the right decision made it possible for me to wipe my eyes and rise to my feet.

There was a knock at the door and Mom peeked her head in. "We saw grandma!" she chirped, and Dad's head popped up just above hers. "On the window sill!" he buzzed, his eyes smiling.

Grandma had died more than a year before. They told me they were standing by Isabelle's bed when Mom spotted the bird, flying at first, then perched on the outside window sill, looking into the room. I immediately understood the bird's significance. In our family, it was a well-known belief that the deceased often made appearances to let the living know they were okay. A bird's body was a natural mode of transportation for a soul.

"It was grandma; I know it was!" Dad said excitedly.

"What kind of bird was it?" I asked them, and they both looked at me, dumbfounded. We weren't avian experts. We knew our robins, blue jays, and cardinals on a good day, but that was the extent of it.

"But she had her head tilted like she was looking at Isabelle," Mom said. "Like she wanted us to know she was ready to bring her to Heaven."

My eyes filled with tears and my vision blurred again. We followed them out of the room to where our family and friends waited just outside of Isabelle's room. I couldn't make out the faces, but I could feel their eyes on me. I felt my sister's hand take mine and I leaned into her, weariness overwhelming me.

"Will you be with me? In the room?" I whispered to her.

She squeezed my hand and I couldn't tell if it was her hand sweating or mine. "Of course," she said.

We filed into Isabelle's room, filling the space to capacity. Pastor Tom urged us to hold hands, then led us in the Lord's Prayer. I closed my eyes and recited the lines out loud. Then one by one each person said their final goodbye to Isabelle and left the room until it was just Chad, Kim, and me, and the nurse and the doctor. The nurse pulled the window curtains to the hallway closed, and the doctor explained that he would remove the tubes and that we could hold Isabelle until she stopped breathing.

"Have you ever—" he paused for the words he thought were right, "—seen someone stop breathing?"

We shook our heads and he explained that it sometimes could take several minutes or even several hours for a person to stop breathing completely when taken off of life support.

"The lungs are very resilient," he explained. "Their job is to keep breathing, and while every other part of the body slowly shuts down they keep trying."

I later learned that this bit of information from the doctor infuriated Chad. If lungs were so resilient, he asked, why hadn't they kept working when Isabelle was at day care?

"How do we know," I whispered. "How do we know that she's going to stop? What if..."

He looked down at his feet. "She'll stop," he said.

It was as if the nurse read my mind, because she said, "We'll be giving her morphine. We don't think she can feel anything, but... just to be certain."

The doctor nodded. "She won't feel anything."

I heard a choking, gasping sound and looked around, then realized it was coming from me. This was the kind of horrid scene from a television show, but this couldn't be real life. *Our* real life. My body went numb again and the doctor's voice grew farther and farther away.

My baby was going to die. And nothing would be the same ever again.

Chad rubbed my knee as I took deep breath after deep breath, afraid that the moment Isabelle stopped breathing, I would stop breathing, too. She had become part of me, the best part of me, and if that part died... Well, it only made sense that I would die, too. I looked to Chad, who also took deep breaths. I rubbed his hand to try to comfort him, but he still looked so stable and strong to me. And here I was perched on the corner of the bench, half on, half off, about to slip into my own puddle on the floor. I couldn't suck out the little bit of energy left in my husband. I wanted him to give that to Isabelle. So, I asked God to help me, to give me strength in my weakness.

Chad reached out for Isabelle when the doctor unhooked her and I was so thankful, again, for his strength. My arms were like putty and I was afraid to hold her, afraid of my own response. The room was warm and she only wore a diaper and the pink socks. I rubbed her skin, loving the feel of its softness on my fingers.

Chad began to talk to Isabelle about Heaven as if he'd been there, and I envisioned the place she was journeying to. Chad told Isabelle about his grandparents, said their names, assured her that they were already there waiting, that it was okay to go to them.

"And if you see a little lady running around bossing everybody and telling them what to do, well, she's ours," said Kim. "That's our grandma. Grandma Florence. She likes to be called Flo."

I found the fortitude to laugh through my tears and so did Chad, who'd only met Grandma Flo once at our wedding. I told Isabelle about all of our puppies and kitties, and Kim helped me remember their names. Then Chad told her about his childhood pets. I felt comforted knowing that she wasn't going alone. Grandma Flo had already arrived, prompt as always, to accompany her on the journey. I looked behind me at the window and the bird was still there. What Isabelle had waiting for her I could only imagine, and the more I tried to imagine Heaven, the more comforted I felt.

After half an hour, Chad and I told Isabelle it was okay to go.

"You tried so hard, baby girl," Chad said, "but mommy and me will be okay. It's time for you to go now. Time to go to Heaven and feel better."

I pressed my hand into my forehead. "It's okay, Isabelle," I whispered. "We'll be okay."

I looked up at Chad, who watched me. I nodded to him. *We'll be okay.*

It took one hour and three minutes, and after Isabelle took her last breath, the doctor sat down next to Chad, held the stethoscope to her chest, and said simply, "She's gone."

The last muscle holding me together gave out and I collapsed onto the floor and cried, a surprisingly soft sob. I felt alternating emotions course through my veins with each sharp thud of my heart, then my mind started to chatter. *How can this be? What is happening here? A feeling of relief? A feeling of warmth and calm? Am I dying? My God, what is going on?* I struggled to understand, but more importantly, push away, the feeling of relief I felt that Isabelle had finally stopped trying to breathe. It was true that, once I knew her fate, I couldn't bear to watch her struggle anymore. I touched Isabelle's face and noticed that her skin glowed a golden hue. She looked perfect, totally at peace. The calm feeling rushed through my body again as if I'd been hooked up to the garden hose of tranquility. I closed my eyes and let the feeling ripple through me. *In our weakness God's strength is made perfect.*

* * *

A representative from LifeSource was waiting in the hallway when we came out of ICU Room No. 2. He asked if our nurse or doctor had talked to us about tissue and organ donation. I bit my lip and turned away.

"No one has talked to us," Chad said plainly.

The LifeSource representative explained the benefits of organ and tissue donation, and said only Isabelle's heart valves would be eligible for the program. I didn't ask why, and after I was able to push aside the images of someone cutting into her little body, I agreed with Chad that if we could help another baby sometime down the road, that would be nice.

"It's just her body," I told Chad an hour later as we waited for the LifeSource rep to make copies of our paperwork. "I mean, her soul's already in Heaven, right?"

Chad's eyes had that distant look he usually reserved for my ramblings about house cleaning and laundry.

I rubbed his hand. "Right?"

He snapped to with a slight head shake. "There just has to be some way to avoid this," he said, his jaw clenched. "Some way to tell if a baby stops breathing before it's too late."

I listened intently as my heartbeat picked up speed. Chad shared with me conversations he'd had with Nurse Chris about how there wasn't anything available on the retail market to detect if a baby stopped moving or stopped breathing.

"You mean like a monitor?" I asked.

"Yeah, like a monitor," Chad said, the distant look back in his eyes.

And just like that my crusade began.

Chapter Ten

Chad and I stayed in Andre's guest bedroom that night. Neither one of us wanted to go home, which was especially sad to me since I loved our house. I feared now that I'd be forced to sell it with the hope that we'd find a new place, a home without memories, where we could start anew.

When I woke the next morning, my eyes yet to open, it was as if I was a blank slate. I didn't know where I was and I felt nothing. Then little by little the details of the last week pummeled me like hail stones. I rolled onto my stomach, smashed my head into my hands, and cried. Chad stirred and leaned over to rub my back. We lay in bed for a long while, neither one of us speaking, but both of us breathing a lot.

I tried to eat the breakfast of scrambled eggs and toast that Andre made, but wound up sitting in the front yard instead, until morning turned into afternoon. The grass was dewy and I sat in it not caring that the wetness seeped through my favorite jeans, dampening my skin. I ran my hand over the recently mowed blades. Each piece was crowned by a diamond-like droplet sparkling wildly in the morning sun, and when the light breeze blew, some droplets clung to the top of the grass while others released and flowed easily down the blades. The irony of this perfect day was not lost on me. I wondered how the clocks could keep ticking. How the moon could still rise, then drop out of sight to make way for the sun? How was I supposed to go on?

By late afternoon, I knew we'd stalled long enough. We couldn't put off the home-going forever. It helped that Mom, Dad, and Kim stayed at our house. It felt less empty that way. They met us outside when we pulled into the driveway. I couldn't get over the perfectly beautiful day, the kind of day that reminded me why I chose to be a

Minnesotan and weather the harsh winters. I sat on the corner of the backyard deck, alert and uncomfortable, unsure if I wanted, or would be able, to enter my own house.

Dad sat next to me.

"This is such a big yard," he said, looking out over the acre of land. This was his first visit since Chad and I had bought the side-by-side duplex four years earlier. We rented out the other side and Dad said he was impressed with all of the remodeling we'd done. Kim had given him an official tour.

"What are all of those molds for in the garage?" he asked and I gave him the lowdown on the 150-plus plaster molds I'd picked up for a steal on Craigslist during a clay-casting phase.

"Where do you have your kiln?" Dad asked. "For your glass bottles?"

"Inside. Laundry room." I said flatly, then led him to the back of our giant garage. "Did you see Chad's workshop?"

Dad nodded and looked around again anyway. "I would have loved a garage like this."

I meandered back to my safe spot on the deck. The world hadn't exploded while I'd sat there earlier, so I figured I'd sit awhile longer. I felt the house looking expectantly over my shoulder, felt it calling my name, begging me to come inside.

Mom and Kim sat with me for awhile, then I gave them a tour of my overgrown vegetable garden and threw Raven's Frisbee until I wore the poor dog out. Then I saw Chad come out of the house looking weary, but unscathed, so I decided it was my turn to go forward into battle. I stepped inside through the door from the deck. It was still my kitchen with the yellow walls, but there was also the faint smell of cleaning chemicals and genetically engineered lemons. My sister had been at work. The dining room looked the same, too, and by the time I'd rounded the corner to the living room, I realized what was different. All of Isabelle's things were gone. Her swing, her toys, her bouncy seat and all of the other baby baubles that often had me referring to our house as "The home built by Fischer Price."

I turned around, and tears spilled from my eyes, bypassing my cheeks to land on the beige carpet of my too-empty living room.

"I had them put everything in Isabelle's room," Chad said from the doorway of the dining room. He took my hand as we went upstairs together to our bedroom, passing by the closed door to Isabelle's room.

We sat carefully on our king-size bed with the king-size furniture that fit so perfectly into the large room. We took turns looking awkwardly at each other. We gazed absently at the dark red walls and stared at the comforter with such intensity that I was sure I could have burned a hole through the dark fabric.

"What are we supposed to do now?" I blurted to Chad and the tears fell again. We lay back on the bed, wrapped tight in each other's arms as we tried to find comfort in a person who needed comforting.

Chad didn't answer me, and after a long silence, he said, "I'm going to take at least a month off from work."

Work hadn't even crossed my mind and in that instant I decided I was done with real estate for good. Towel in. I was out. Life was too damn short.

"I think we should go to Hawaii," Chad said.

"Okay," I agreed and Chad rose to his arm to look at me.

"Seriously?" he asked and I could tell he was shocked and wondered if my response was the result of shock, too.

"Whatever," I said.

Chad rolled onto his back. "You wouldn't be afraid to fly?"

I shook my head. "I'm not afraid of anything anymore." And I meant it. My fear of flying, fear of elevators, fear of overly crowded places, and one billion other fears that had limited us not only on our travel excursions, but also in our day-to-day activities, seemed to be gone.

The start of a smile curled at the corners of Chad's lips at the prospect of visiting Hawaii, a destination I knew he'd always wanted to visit. It was nice to see him smile, so I told him to double-check with my sister to make sure she could come and to book the tickets. I didn't care about the cost. We had a little money in our Rainy Day fund and this was the tsunami from hell. Plus, I was done worrying about money and all of the other stuff I couldn't control.

Our brief moment of serenity was cut short when we descended the stairs to find our families, Pastor Tom, and Interim Pastor Linda huddled together in our dining room. Just like the movies, they grew quiet and still when we entered and I resisted the urge to look over my shoulder to see if the Sunnybrook Institution van was parked in the driveway. Were they still worried I was going to kill myself?

"We need to talk about the funeral," Mom said and touched my arm lightly.

I heard someone whisper "funeral home," and someone else mention "casket," and with that I summoned Chad out onto the deck.

"I don't want her buried in the ground," I told him. "I don't want a wake with people gawking at her. I don't want her put in the ground."

I prepared myself for battle but it wasn't necessary. Chad nodded and quickly agreed that we could have Isabelle cremated. No one in his family had ever been cremated, but he understood my perspective. We would find a beautiful container of some sort, not an urn per say, and we'd keep her ashes in the living room where they would always be close to us.

Chad's sister, Andre, made the phone call to the funeral home and we filed into the building an hour later. The funeral director was clearly overwhelmed by the number of people and struggled to find seats for all of us. I felt bad for him at first, but as he went through the motions of planning a funeral—cold as ice—my sympathy vanished. I half listened to him while I found solace in my flip-flops. Then he started to talk about the rate per line for obituaries in the local newspaper and Andre insisted he stop.

"Can we talk about the costs later?" she asked, motioning to Chad and me.

"Well, it's part of the process—" he bristled.

"You can talk to us," Chad's mom said, and pointed to my mom. "After we're done here."

He left the room to type up our paperwork and Pastor Tom apologized for the man's insensitive nature.

"I'm sorry, too, you guys," Andre said, perched on the edge of her seat. "When we planned Neal's dad's funeral, they were so nice and caring. This guy's a jerk!"

There was chit-chat among our families about the funeral director's demeanor. "He does this for a living, but needs to remember his manners," someone said.

Pastor Tom interrupted. "Let's talk about Isabelle."

I was stunned into looking up. As abrupt as his comment was, there was something so soothing about Pastor Tom. For the next half an hour, we shared our favorite memories of Isabelle. I said that I loved the way she calmed down whenever I played the Bee Gees.

"I love that she made us morning people," Chad said. "One of my favorite things was slipping into her room in the morning to catch her playing with her bears."

Jennie dropped by the house almost daily to get her "Izzy Fix," and Andre loved pretending Isabelle was one of her own children when they went out to dinner or to one of the kids' baseball games. We shared stories and memories and laughed and cried, and when the funeral director came back into the room, we continued to share until we were finished.

The funeral was two days later, on Sunday, and it was another sunny day. I was pissed. The least God could have done was give me a little rain. The sun felt like a slap in the face. As visitors trickled into Cross of Peace where we held the service, I felt increasingly sick to my stomach that this nightmare really was my new life. Our families had created four large poster boards on which they displayed dozens of pictures of Isabelle, along with cute baby stickers, phrases, and poems titled "A Child Loaned" and "God's Way." After visitors looked at the pictures, they inevitably looked at me—and I couldn't stand their gazes of pity or, even worse, their forced smiles. I guessed that they felt sad, but more than anything they probably felt grateful that they weren't in my shoes. With that in mind, finding the wherewithal to thank everybody for coming took every last bit of energy from my body.

"Do you know all of these people?" Dad asked as the church filled to capacity and volunteers scurried to set up chairs in the lobby and hallway.

I nodded and scanned the room. There were coworkers, friends, Chad's relatives from Iowa, distant acquaintances I hadn't seen for years… I sat down on the bench. *All of these people came to support us,* I thought. *On a gorgeous Sunday when they could have done half-a-dozen other things that lifted rather than lowered their spirits…they came here.*

My irritation turned to gratitude and that may have been what got me through the funeral. That, and my sister next to me holding my hand when the Bee Gees' songs, "To Love Somebody" and "How Deep Is Your Love," came through the church's overhead speakers. I guessed it was the first time the Bee Gees had performed at Cross of Peace, and hot tears poured out of my eyes as Pastor Tom explained Isabelle's affinity for the music to the crowd of 250-plus people.

Somehow, after the service I found the strength to amble from table to table to thank those who came to celebrate Isabelle's life. It felt strangely reminiscent of the tour Chad and I took around the reception hall after our wedding; many of the same people were present, but there were no congratulations or cheers of excitement.

The church's "Helping Hands" group prepared and served a nice lunch, which was helpful since I hadn't thought twice about feeding people. Luckily our families had thought twice and took care of the details. The truth was, I hadn't thought about much of anything for a week except breathing and trying to keep something, usually a fruit smoothie, in my stomach. I thanked God for my caretakers.

At the end of the afternoon, I finally crumpled into a metal church chair where a table full of my high school friends gathered, including Jen and Marti. They continued with a conversation and didn't stop to stare at me, which I appreciated. By coming to this funeral, they had silently agreed to share a piece of my life that extended beyond algebra class and locker assignments. And in the coming weeks, months, and years, the people in my life would each react differently to the news of Isabelle's death. Some would gather close to me as these friends did. Some would approach tentatively, unsure of how to act around me. And still others would step out of my life completely, seemingly terrified that tragedy might be contagious.

Chapter Eleven

Somehow a week passed, Dad went back to Florida, and Kim would leave in three days. Mom planned to stay for another week-and-a-half. Chad busied himself with a woodworking project in the garage; it distracted him from the pain. I checked on him often. It gave me something to do other than look at myself in the bathroom mirror and wonder for the umpteenth time if this was really my life.

"That's going to be nice," I said, rubbing my hand along the bench seat he was building. It would have a bead-board backing with coat hooks, a spot for shoes below, and I would paint it white. I had made a drawing several months before based on an entryway structure I saw in a home remodeling magazine, and he followed it precisely. Too precisely, I thought, as I watched him work. I'd drawn in two shelves for our shoes, one of the shelves scaled down to hold the tiniest of shoes. I put my hand over my mouth as familiar sobs bubbled in my throat.

Chad noticed, glanced at the shelf, then looked back at me. "I know," he said, and closed his eyes as the storm rumbled in again.

He reached for me, and at the same moment, a yellow and white butterfly breezed into the garage, darted mere inches from my face, dipped down around my legs, and landed on my right ankle. I gasped, looked up at Chad and smiled. I felt its tiny legs tickle my skin, a delightful sensation. I bent slightly from the waist for a better look, which must have startled the butterfly, because she flapped her delicate wings and sailed away. I wanted to chase her, but I didn't. I held tight to that moment and it got me through the next few days.

* * *

Somehow I functioned. I got up every morning, dressed, sometimes brushed my hair (even though the short style rarely required more than a quick rake of my fingers), brushed my teeth, and even had a little appetite now and then. Mom and Kim talked me in to displaying my melted glass at the city's street fair that weekend. I'd paid for the booth space months before and Kim organized the layout and setup. I had a moment of strength and I agreed to participate in what was traditionally a fun family event. But I knew the moment we got the not-so-easy E-Z-Up tent erected that the whole thing was a mistake. It was too soon for something like this. My nerve endings were still exposed. Everywhere I looked I saw babies and families and pregnant bellies. I even saw a girl from our birth prep class with her baby. I felt enraged at the sight of her and her living child.

I walked to the end of the block, out of the thick of things, and saw a mother charging well ahead of a little girl, snapping at her over her should to "speed it up." Then, on the other side of the street, I saw a parent pulling her son too hard by his skinny little arm. My ears buzzed with the voices of parents yelling at children who clearly only wanted to partake in the fun of the festival with a corn dog, cotton candy, or a ticket for the ring toss game.

Chad and I left the booth in my sister's capable hands, took another walk, and compared notes. We both had "it."

"It's…it's like, almost like an empty feeling," Chad said, frustrated with his inability to find the right words. I knew what he meant. I felt it, too. I had more words for it than I wanted, though.

"It's like a cavernous hole that's growing deeper and deeper every day we don't have her, and I'm afraid that soon it'll be so large that we'll fall inside ourselves and we'll be lost to the rest of the world forever." I paused. "How will we ever get out of this? How will we ever be normal again?"

Chad reached for my hand and we walked. He had his sunglasses on so I couldn't see his eyes, but I saw the smirk at the corner of his mouth. "A cavernous hole, huh?"

I pushed into him as we walked and squeezed his hand. It felt good to have someone to hold on to.

* * *

On Aug. 1, the I-35W bridge that crossed the Mississippi River in Minneapolis collapsed, killing 13 people and injuring 145. The entire metro area was on high alert and our news stations ran continuous footage of the catastrophe. I knew I wasn't thinking rationally and I chastised myself as I sat in the living room and watched the footage on T.V. I silently cursed the reporters who gave so much attention to the bridge collapse and to the volunteers who tried to help by plunging into the river in search of life. Hadn't anyone heard my baby died? Couldn't the world just stand still for a few days and let me catch my breath before I was expected to have sympathy for others?

In the bathtub that evening, I thought about the monitoring system Chad had mentioned in the hospital. *Why can't I start a company? Why can't I create a monitor that could save babies' lives?* I wondered if I could prevent other parents from experiencing the heart-wrenching pain I couldn't escape. *What if that is it? A baby monitor. What if that is the purpose behind our tragedy? I mean, there has to be a purpose, right? God wouldn't just take Isabelle from us for no reason, would he?*

* * *

Chad and I were shocked that people sent us money. Our family members assured us that the tradition of sending cash was common when a death occurred. Yet, neither one of us had ever experienced a death that was close enough to warrant sympathy cards let alone checks, cash, and, in one case, a Target gift card. Most of the cards people sent had hand-written messages saying something like, "We're praying for you," or ,"You're in our prayers."

One card in particular had a saying that I would later end up posting on my wall at work to refer to daily: "I shall think of her as smiling…for what else would one do in the presence of God."

It was comforting to read the cards over and over again, but I wondered whether the majority of people really did pray or if it was just something to say when they didn't know what to say. I continued to tiptoe around my relationship with God. Being an organized person, I wanted to define my role with him and wondered if I could really count on him unconditionally.

I made an announcement to Mom about God a few nights before she flew back to Florida, and it felt like a coming-out-of-the-closet kind of event.

"I prayed a lot," I told her over spaghetti. "Talked to God. At the hospital. I might keep doing it."

I didn't look up and Mom didn't comment. She probably sensed this was something I needed to work out on my own. I didn't know if I could ever get over the fact that I felt like God had a lot of making up to do, that he owed me after taking something so valuable. Maybe I'd come around. Maybe someday I'd accept what Pastor Tom suggested, that God doesn't pull strings. But I was sure he had the power, the ability to heal Isabelle, so why hadn't he? Why had he chosen to let her die?

A few nights later, Chad announced he was having Carla and her husband over to our house "to talk."

"I'm not so sure about that," I told Chad, afraid of what my reaction would be when I saw Carla.

"She's grieving, too, and needs to have some kind of closure," he said, and I was glad he was so level-headed. There was a part of me that was sure I would be fine if I never saw her again.

I sure as heck didn't expect to hug her, which was what I did when she showed up at the front door, her eyes swollen and her cheeks red. Chad led Carla and her husband, Bryan, onto our deck overlooking the back yard.

The first thing Carla asked was if we blamed her.

"A little," Chad said and I appreciated his candor. He told her that we were working through our feelings and didn't have anyone else to blame. She was our only target. She was the last person to see Isabelle alive.

Chad and I had "what-if'd" ourselves into madness in the hospital thinking that if Carla had checked on Isabelle she could have prevented the whole thing, but Chad—again so damn level-headed—reminded me repeatedly of the half-hour or hour-long naps Isabelle had taken at home, and how we rarely checked on her until we heard her stir or cry through the sound monitor.

After a little bit of talking, my heart softened toward Carla. I couldn't stay angry at her. I revealed that there was a part of me that was strangely thankful I'd taken Isabelle to day care that day.

"You are?" she asked, her face reading stunned and stupefied.

"If it had happened here—" I sucked in a huge breath of air, "—if Isabelle had stopped breathing here, I don't know what I would have done." I dropped my head into my hands. "Not that I know what I'm going to do now…"

Carla started to cry again. "I'm not thankful you brought her to my house," she said and broke into full-on sobs.

I felt another glimmer of sympathy for her. I saw the situation from her perspective, and like my perspective, it was dark and sad and overwhelming. I felt harsh now that I had instructed my family not to allow Carla to approach me at the funeral. In fact, I had asked my family not to allow her to come to the funeral at all, but Chad had argued that I was being unfair.

Later that evening, Carla brought me Isabelle's things that had been stored in her cubby at day care: diapers, wipes, A & D ointment, and a pink sundress in case she messed up her other clothes. Chad took the garbage bag full of items upstairs. I heard him open Isabelle's door, set the bag down, then shut the door. The floor hadn't given its familiar creak, so I knew he hadn't stepped inside her room. Maybe just stretched from the doorway.

Carla reached into her purse and pulled out the check I had given her for the week Isabelle should have been at day care.

"You didn't cash it?" I asked, knowing that the Monday morning ritual usually involved Carla piling the kids into her Suburban for a trip to the bank and sometimes McDonald's PlayLand. I always thought that Isabelle probably enjoyed those little field trips with all of her friends.

"You never signed it," she said, handing me the check.

I took it from her. Sure enough, I hadn't. A strange sensation tingled through my body. It was unlike me to leave a light on inside the house when I left, let alone a signature off a check. I'd become hyper-vigilant to events surrounding Isabelle's death and had frequently wondered if there were signs I'd foolishly missed. Signs that could have changed her fate. But I chalked the unsigned check up to a coincidence. What else could it have been?

That night I visited Isabelle's room. I felt good about the time we'd spent with Carla and her husband, and I felt confident as I walked up the stairs. I opened the door and the sweet smell of Isabelle tickled my nose. I crumpled to the floor. I crawled out of the room and into the hallway, pulling the door closed behind me. I wasn't quick enough, though. Sadness covered me like a thick coat of black paint. I cried on the hallway floor until exhaustion set in and I had no choice but to retreat to our bedroom.

* * *

Chad's dad offered us his frequent flyer miles to buy plane tickets. He agreed that getting out of our familiar surroundings might be good for us. The miles weren't good for flights to Hawaii, though, so Chad did all of the planning for a trip to the Florida Keys. He'd taken the month of August off of work and I didn't think twice about not checking my real estate e-mail or voicemail accounts.

We received enough money from the cards that came in the mail to pay for our retreat from reality. I was beside myself with gratitude, especially since I hadn't expected a penny. Chad's friends from high school went in together and surprised us with a Visa gift card to take on our trip. Chad's mom sent out thank you notes to the people she knew, but I couldn't bring myself to send any out. I felt guilty, an emotion that had taken up residence on my sleeve, and I hoped that people didn't really *expect* "thank you's" considering the circumstances. It was a huge undertaking for me just to go through the mail and see that the bills got paid.

We used the money to rent a two-story oceanside villa in Marathon Key for ten days. My sister and her boyfriend planned to drive the four hours south to stay with us for a few days, Mom and her boyfriend planned to visit for a couple of days, and our friends Joe and Leslie, who would be at their timeshare in Miami that week, also planned to come for a day or two. There was no denying that Chad and I left very few holes in our schedule for time alone together. We'd spent the three weeks since Isabelle's death sucking what little life we could find out of each other just to keep going. We didn't verbalize our fears, but it was obvious we both worried that, if left alone in a place where we didn't have our own corners to hide in or personal objects to distract us, our pain might bounce so powerfully off of the walls that we'd both be knocked out. I hoped that our guests could infuse in us a little bit of their positive energy.

The villa was stunning, with ocean views from our two balconies. The pastel, beachy décor was so different from my shabby chic furnishings at home, and the change of scenery was bittersweet. We snorkeled, we jet skied, we ate dinner at fancy and not-so-fancy restaurants, and we lounged in hammocks. I read books, magazines, and the resort directory to keep my mind occupied. Chad had brought his Wii, so on the few nights when it rained, he battled with my mom and sister in bowling matches. I took a picture of him smiling in front of the T.V. with a high score of 298. It was refreshing to see him smile.

During one of the evenings we were alone together, Chad and I talked about Heaven and what we thought it might be like. I remembered my confirmation instructor saying that what happens to our souls when we die *surpasses human understanding.* Nearly twenty years later, that thought comforted me. It removed the burden of trying to figure it all out.

"Will Isabelle grow up in Heaven?" I asked Leslie a few days later as we sat on the deck of the villa. She was reading an article in *Self* magazine as I flipped absently through the pages of Oprah's *O* magazine.

Leslie shook her head. "People don't age in Heaven," she said without looking up, and I thought it was interesting that those I asked tended to have pretty definitive ideas of what Heaven would be like.

Still, the question of Heaven occupied my thoughts.

"If I don't die until I'm eighty-eight, I'll look different," I told Chad as we floated around the resort pool on Funnoodles. "How will Isabelle know me?"

"She'll just know," he said, and after some thought, added, "We'll probably see Isabelle as we remember her, and she'll see us as she remembers us." He hugged me. "And, we'll see each other as old farts."

We splashed around and tried to make light of a very heavy topic. My mind reeled with more questions, and I wondered what people did all day in Heaven and if God gave them jobs. Did they have little houses and little cars? Or did they fly everywhere? Eventually, exhausted by my own imagination, I let the questions bead and roll off of my sunscreen-laden skin. It was hard to give myself up to God, to really trust that he could possibly have my best interests in mind after all that had happened. That day, though, I trusted him about 90 percent. I even asked God to continue to take good care of Isabelle and I asked him to make sure she watched me. *Every time she sees me smile and laugh, it's because I know I will see her someday soon and that's what keeps me afloat.*

* * *

Near the end of our trip, we stayed in Key West one night with Mom and her boyfriend at a Days Inn Hotel. I woke up at 6:30 a.m., ventured across the street to the Waffle House, had breakfast alone, and wrote lines of poetry and a letter to God in my journal.

Saturday, September 1

Why did you let me meet her?
Love her?
Reshape my life around her?
Why did you teach me to be flexible?
To meet her demands?
To put her first and put myself aside?
To give in to her every whim?
Finally giving me a purpose.
Why did you make her laugh so sweet
that I was suckered in like candy?
And her smile so big that I was overwhelmed by my own desire to
touch her little lips again and again?
And why did you make her eyes so deep
that she was able to see right through me?
Why—oh WHY!—would you take her from me
at the moment I fully found her and finally found myself?
I want to believe she's at home with you now,
and I can't have her back.
But I deserve some sort of answer…
God, please give me that.

* * *

Dear God,

Did you know? She'll sleep through the night if you give her a bottle before bed. She loves having her diaper changed when we wind up the bear mobile next to her changing table. She likes to watch them go round and round and round. She squeals with delight.

If you sneak into her room in the morning, she'll probably be awake— just laying there, waiting for you. And even though you intend to surprise her, she'll surprise you with her smiles and her wiggles. And all it will take is a smile from you and you'll set off her giggles.

P.S.: If there are doors in Heaven, don't WD40 Isabelle's. She knows that the creaking of the door means someone is coming to get her.

Tears rolled down my cheeks as the waitress delivered my waffles, topped beautifully with strawberries and whipped cream.

"You okay, honey?" she asked and I nodded.

Thankfully she didn't pry. I managed to eat half of the breakfast and then went to the hotel lobby to watch the morning news.

Television news didn't typically interest me, but there was some crazy story about a politician who touched another guy's foot under a bathroom stall and wound up resigning from his position because of all of the insinuations that he was soliciting sex. I was intrigued. The next story on the news was about breastfeeding versus bottle feeding and the rest of the room faded away as the news anchor demanded my full attention. The story was very one-sided and, with the anchor's final words, my vision went blurry. The snippet claimed that not breastfeeding your child for at least six months increased the baby's risk of SIDS. I jumped off the couch and walked around the building until I found the swimming pool.

God! Isn't it bad enough that I spent my first month-and-a-half drowning in postpartum depression and lost my daughter? Now you're telling me I'm the one to blame for her death! What are the chances of that story being on? I rarely watch TV and have never watched TV in a hotel lobby before. Are you giving me a sign? Are you telling me it's my fault?

I sat down on a dirty plastic lounge chair, tried to cry, but no tears came. I needed tears. I needed to sob. I needed to get the awful feeling out of me. It was thick and consuming and I recognized it by name: *Guilt.* I felt guilty for not breastfeeding Isabelle and I felt especially guilty that morning for telling her I hated her.

I slapped at my chest. *Is that why she died? Did she feel like I didn't want her?* I wondered if God took her away because I was unfit. Did he look down at me and say, "Oh man, I made a mistake this time. I better get that poor baby out of there."

I wallowed in my own murky pool of self-loathing for a good half hour before I went back to the room, broke down, and told Chad and Mom that Isabelle's death was my fault.

Chad shook his head like he thought I was overreacting, and Mom poo-pooed me and told me to get my things together. I didn't move, just stared at her. She tucked her curling iron inside her bag and came to stand next to me.

"I want to hold her, Mom," I cried, and buried my face in her shoulder.

She rubbed my back and it was comforting enough to bring the ache in my chest down a few notches. But I knew Mom wouldn't be there to rub my back when we went home to Minnesota and I wanted something permanent to memorialize Izzy, some way to keep her close to me that I could see and touch.

Chapter Twelve

We arrived at Key West Ink tattoo shop and I felt oddly eager to be pricked repeatedly with a sharp needle. It would be a pain I could understand. Chad would have Isabelle's baptism portrait tattooed on his chest, including the cross necklace she'd worn, and her name scripted below. I would have her favorite orange ring, the first toy she'd learned to clutch and later squealed for, printed forever on my right ankle. Her name would be scripted in the same font as Chad's on a banner weaving through the toy. I intended to wait the three hours it would take for the tattoo artist to complete Chad's tattoo, so he could work his magic on me.

I made myself comfy in the waiting area while Boe, a biker-looking guy with a shaved head and Hulk Hogan mustache, shaved the few hairs from Chad's chest and used some sort of carbon copy paper method to transfer his drawing onto Chad's skin. His drawing was amazing and I hoped, hoped, hoped, that the actual tattoo would look as good. The last thing I wanted was a baby who didn't look like Isabelle forever imprinted on my husband's chest.

"You need something?" asked a girl with black hair, tattoos on all of her exposed skin and a variety of piercings.

I shook my head. "My husband's getting a tattoo."

"You want one?"

I tried to be patient but I was in no mood to be sold. "Yes," I said. "I'm getting one. As soon as Boe's done with my husband."

She shook her head. "That's going to take hours, probably four or five—"

"Three," I said.

"Whatever." She pulled out a sketch pad and pencil. "I'll do your tattoo. Boe doesn't have time for you today. He's got other appointments coming in."

"I am his other appointment." I tried to sound stern but the truth was she sort of scared me. She had a tattoo on her upper arm of a vixen-devil figure with the word "Unlovable" underneath, and she had barbed wire tattooed around her wrists.

"Boe asked me to help him out because he's busy today," she insisted and like a little wimp, I folded.

"All right," I said and handed her Boe's drawing of my tattoo.

"Great!" she said, bouncing once on the couch. "I'm Pixie."

Pixie instructed me to sit in her chair while she banged drawers and flipped items around until she found what she needed. It didn't even help that my cat's name was Pixie. I felt no connection to this girl and it seemed I should at least feel some connection to the person who would create my tattoo in Isabelle's memory. I looked around for help. Chad was five bays away in a reclined position while Boe, wearing magnifying glasses over his eyes, chiseled away at my husband's skin. I wanted to yell to him, *Boe! Boe! Help me! Don't let her touch me!* but he was busy at work. I figured if he let this Pixie work in his shop, she had to have some skills.

I didn't look at my tattoo once during the half hour it took Pixie to create her "masterpiece." Instead, I closed my eyes and thought about the day I took Isabelle to an art fair by the lake. It was the beginning of June and the air was hot and thick. She was dressed in a red and white checkered sundress with Elmo embroidered on the tiny front pocket. She wore a matching hat that made her chubby cheeks look even more plump than they were. We enjoyed a light lunch by the lake and she stretched out on a blanket in the shade afterward. It was one of the first days I felt good after the weight of the postpartum depression lifted. It was a memory I had returned to several times, wishing I had spent more time with her on that blanket, squeezed her just a little bit tighter, and drank in her scent just a little bit longer.

"I'm done!" Pixie announced, yanking me from my memory.

I looked down. Of course my skin was swollen and red, I expected that, but there was also a thick black line around Izzy's orange ring, and the scripted letters of Isabelle's name didn't connect to each other like cursive writing should.

I looked up at her.

"Looks good, doesn't it?" she asked, slapping a thick layer of petroleum jelly over my ankle. She covered it with plastic wrap and tape.

I wanted to cry and I felt the tears well on my lids.

"Oh, it'll only hurt for a few hours," she said. "I can't believe you're being such a baby now. The hard part's over." She cocked her head. "Who's Isabelle anyway?"

My cheeks became the waterslide for the tears pouring from my eyes. I pushed off the seat, my legs making a schlocking noise as the black vinyl released its sticky hold. I was two steps away from the bathroom when Pixie yelled, "Hold it!"

I turned around and put my hand to my mouth.

"Seriously, hold it," she said. "I forgot to run down to the Dollar Store to get toilet paper."

I didn't know where to go, and Chad and Boe were still engrossed in his tattoo. I hustled to the waiting area and rifled through my purse where I kept a supply of tissues.

"So, who did you say Isabelle was?" Pixie yelled over to me and I saw Chad in the wall-length mirror turn his head.

"My daughter," I said and blew my nose.

I could feel Pixie's stare and when I looked up, her dark eyes were still on me.

"She passed away," I finally said, hoping for the first time that my words would make someone feel badly for asking.

Pixie dramatically dropped a plastic bottle of cleaning solution to the floor, approached me and sat adjacent to me in the leather chair. "I lost someone recently, too," she said and didn't meet my eyes. "It almost killed me."

My heart kicked out two extra beats and I wondered if that was why I'd come into contact with this awful creature. Were we kindred spirits? Was I here to help her? Or was she here to help me? Or better yet, was there someone who could help both of us?

"My dog," she said flatly and started to cry. "Can I have one of those?" She pointed to my tissues.

"Your dog?" I asked and hoped, for her sake, that I hadn't heard her right.

"I'd had him since I was twelve, and when my parents kicked me out at sixteen, I took him with me and I moved to Key West; and then I became my sister's legal guardian when I turned eighteen—"

she sucked in a shaky breath and rammed the tissue into the corners of her eyes, black eyeliner staining the white material. "She's having a lot of problems with drugs and, I mean, I think she's sleeping around a lot; she's only thirteen, but I'm trying to keep her on the straights, so I'm working as much as I can." She held out her hand and wiggled her fingers for another tissue and I handed her one. "Anyhoo, Baxter died like a month ago and I really felt like he was the only one keeping us together. So, I totally know how you feel." She stood up, threw her tissues into the wastebasket, opened the cash register and pulled out a ten. "Boe! I'm going to get T.P. You need anything?"

Boe looked up and shook his head. He was more than halfway finished with Chad's tattoo and I could see that Isabelle had nearly come to life on the skin that covered Chad's heart. I went outside, found a hiding spot in the alley next to the building, and bawled.

* * *

When we arrived home from the Keys, I struggled with the stories and advice I received in person, via e-mail, and through a couple of "Thinking of You" cards from friends of friends. I became frustrated one evening and vented to Chad.

"Have people really thought about what happened to us? I mean, *really* thought about it? We lost a child, a baby!"

Chad nodded and didn't say anything, but the tears sparkled on the lower lids of his eyes and he hugged me tight. It certainly wasn't fair to compare our loss to the death of a ninety-four-year-old grandmother from natural causes or the horrors of going through a divorce—but, unfortunately, those were the sorts of things people felt compelled to tell me about. And not just that—they often provided detailed game plans for how they got through it, as if I could do the same. Rather than bolstering my spirits as they probably intended, their words made me feel even more alone. Were there other parents out there who'd lost babies like this and, if so, how did they move forward?

I became increasingly introspective in those first few months and tried to make sense of my situation—and the human race, for that matter. I was baffled. Nothing unnerved me more than to hear about someone else's past-due crisis in the wake of my tragedy. I didn't want to deny them their pain. It was real. But I also didn't want the comparisons. It was unfair. And it was in those first months that I imagined a coffee-table book I'd write someday called, *What Not to Say When You Don't Know What to Say*. With anger heavily guiding my thoughts, Chapter One would be titled, "Shut Up, Why Don't You?" and Chapter Two would be titled, "Believe It or Not, This Isn't About You."

My sister told me she'd heard anger was an emotion often experienced during the first months of the grieving process. She gently suggested that maybe I was entering that stage. I had to admit that my fuse did seem surprisingly short, and according to the Kubler-Ross "Five Stages of Grief" handout the hospital had given us, anger came right after denial, which I'd experienced in the hospital. But I wondered if that meant I had bargaining and depression left before I'd eventually move into acceptance. I couldn't imagine ever accepting Isabelle's death. And, I'd experienced bargaining and depression in the hospital as well, so what did that say about my timeline? Had I completely screwed up the steps and now had no promise of recovery? Would I be on this Grief Merry-Go-Round for the rest of my life? And what did recovery mean, really? I wanted Isabelle back and that couldn't happen, so did that mean I would never recover?

Years later, I would be thankful that, in those first few months, I felt driven to immerse myself in Isabelle. I easily could have tried another path, avoided all mention of her, but I didn't. My heart wouldn't let me. We hung her large baptism picture above the T.V., and placed her ashes on the top shelf of the entertainment center in a quaint daisy container Mom and Kim had picked up at a local antique shop. The shelf also became home to her three favorite toys, including the orange ring that was incorporated into my tattoo. I had an "Angel of Remembrance" Willow figurine, a Pearly Gates Precious Moments statue, dried flowers from funeral floral arrangements, and framed pictures of Chad and me with Isabelle.

After the funeral, my sister had instructed those who wanted to send flowers to send a plant that I could repot. Chad hung shelves in the dining room and we wound up with twenty-three pots of fascinating foliage. And as the tendrils of the golden pathos lengthened (I called one of them Rapunzel because I had to trim her vines back only a month after I'd repotted her), I rooted and replanted the clippings, then passed them on to family members and friends in remembrance of Isabelle. The plants needed a fair amount of care with watering, trimming, and repotting. They occupied my time, and having something to take care of made me feel like a part of Isabelle was still alive and growing.

* * *

I've loved to read ever since a special education teacher named Mrs. Nelson taught me how to sound out words, finally, in second grade. I was teased in elementary school before that, and once I'd learned how to read, I went overboard trying to prove to everyone that I was capable. I developed a habit of reading each and every thing that came in front of my eyes—from books, magazines, and newspapers to coupon clippers and restaurant menus. Yet, I had absolutely no interest in reading the grieving books that wound up in our house. I let them pile up on our kitchen table until one afternoon I finally got curious. I flipped open a book titled *How to Survive the Loss of a Child,* and read in the first few pages that grievers should not make any major changes in the first year after a death. I closed the book. But major changes were already on the way for me. I could feel it in my bones.

That night I fidgeted nervously in my seat at the dining room table and fiddled with my plate of spaghetti—the first meal I'd cooked in over a month.

"I'm done with real estate for good," I finally said to Chad, my heart thumping excitedly at the admission. "Life's too short to hate what I'm doing. Maybe I'll write more."

Chad looked at me, big, brown eyes blank, then got another piece of French bread and finished his spaghetti. He'd never been a big conversationalist, I knew that, and I sometimes wished that we could become wrapped up in the kinds of conversations that made some people lose all track of time. As I sat across from him I wished he could find at least a few words in response to my announcement. It was an important decision, and one that, despite the finality of it, made me feel like there might be a new beginning on the horizon for me. Of course, if I was honest with myself, there probably wasn't much Chad could have said about my decision. I had a tendency to puff up like a blow fish if I didn't get my way. And, I usually called the shots around our household. Chad didn't argue because, he'd once said, "It's easier not to argue when I know you've made up your mind."

I quit real estate, I repeated several times to myself that night as I curled into bed with one of Isabelle's blankets pulled to my chest.

Even if I hadn't made the official announcement to my boss, the people who really mattered knew, and that was, after all, all that really mattered. I felt a little rebellious having gone against the grieving book's number one recommendation—no major changes in the first year—but what was the worst that could happen to me? As far as I was concerned, the worst had already bulldozed its way into our life and took Isabelle with it.

* * *

I was home alone one rainy afternoon in September when a lady named "Connie from the County" dropped by unannounced. I saw through the window that she had the body shape of a weeble-wobble and, when I opened the front door, she completely invaded my personal space with her large frame. I knew it wasn't right to judge people, but I didn't like anything about her—from her overbearing demeanor to the tightly wound curls of her short, dark hair. Without a proper greeting, she quickly explained that the county's social services department sends her to parents' houses "in cases like this."

In my dining room, she emptied the contents of a manila envelope onto the table. My fingers twitched as I scanned the pamphlets that appeared to be written by experts on the topic of child loss. I winced when I spied a somber-looking book titled, *SIDS and Infant Death Survival Guide*.

Connie motioned for me to sit and I sank into the chair across from her. Tears welled, not so much because of the grief, but because my home had once again become my sanctuary. But this woman's presence had just cut a hole in my shelter, and the shreds of steadiness I'd maintained over the last few weeks blew right out the top.

As Connie asked questions about "the incident," which I reminded her had already been discussed with the police detective at the hospital, I wondered what kind of sensitivity training people like her went through and if maybe they wouldn't benefit from my *What Not to Say* book.

"Have you thought at all about having other children?" she asked and my arm hairs bristled. She took a breath, then said, "Gosh, I wonder what the rate of SIDS is in subsequent siblings? Humph. That's interesting." Her chunky fingers flipped through pages of paperwork and I noticed that the plump skin on her finger dipped into the valley created by her wedding ring.

I hated that I was just another bereaved parent on her to-do list, and she didn't even look up to see my horrified expression before she added, "Subsequent siblings—" then jotted a note on her yellow notepad and finished, "—that's sort of scary, actually."

I was openly rude to her after that, but not quite rude enough to demand that she leave. Instead, I took on the blasé attitude of a teenager when she asked me more questions. She quickly caught on and excused herself, but not before Raven bounded across the kitchen and leaped at her. Connie weebled and she wobbled, but she didn't fall down.

"Oh, geez," I said and reached for Raven's collar.

"I'll just let myself out," Connie said as she headed toward the front door.

"Okay, then," I said and gave a curt wave over my shoulder as I took my dog into the other room. Raven hadn't jumped up on anyone since she was a puppy, and when I heard Connie close the front door behind her, I ruffled Raven's thick hair around her neck and gave her a treat.

Later, I shoved the books and packet to the corner of the table with the other pieces of literature Chad and I had received. I called my sister, who got especially irate when I told her about the "*Survival Guide.*"

"It seems like an oxymoron written by morons," I said. "SIDS Survival Guide. Doesn't that seem hugely inappropriate for a book title? It's not like we're going camping."

* * *

At the beginning of September, Chad went back to work and there were many afternoons I wandered the dining room, gazing at Isabelle's plants and wondering if she were ever really here at all. I would then move to the living room where I'd sit in front of the shrine we'd created. Each time, angst formed a thick lump in my throat, and if I wanted to cry, I did. Sometimes I bellowed. I talked out loud and when Raven heard my voice, she shuffled over to sit in front of me and I stroked the fur around her neck. It helped to have something to touch. My arms felt empty, and I longed for the weight of my baby.

Chad didn't always make it through the whole day at work, which rattled me because I'd grown accustomed to his unwavering strength. His consistency was one of my favorite things about him. I had once told my mother that Chad was like the stationary planet in our universe—always in the same location with only mild temperature fluctuations—while I felt like a renegade star spiraling around him at breakneck speeds, bouncing off him into another orbit, my lights flickering on and off. Mom had laughed and said we complemented each other well.

So his struggle now spoke to me of the severity of our loss and the frightening path ahead of us. On the days he came home early, he looked drained of color, his blue Walgreens shirt untucked, and his tie loose and crooked like he'd been pulling at it, trying to lessen the grip grief had on him. He cried and got mad and put his hand over his heart—the spot where Isabelle's tattoo was—and he told me how much he missed her. There were times when I was strong and I held him tight while he cried, but more often than not I fell apart too. Other times Chad was the steadfast one, and he rubbed my back and pulled me close with my snotty nose and shaky body while I questioned our future.

I knew there was no secret recipe, but I looked anyway. I Googled "losing an infant" and came up with Web sites and a forum for bereaved parents. I found a Web site called "First Candle," formerly the "SIDS Alliance," and read pages and pages of information about SIDS. I learned there were more than 2,500 SIDS deaths each year in the United States. I followed a link to another site that said the classifications for SIDS deaths were being reorganized, which meant the number was likely closer to 5,000 deaths per year. Sometimes, the site said, the death was classified under "Death from Asphyxia" or "Sudden Unexplained Infant Death" rather than "Sudden Infant Death Syndrome." The reasons were murky. Sometimes there was a blanket in the crib or a stuffed animal, and I wondered if the experts even knew the difference.

We got Isabelle's death certificate the next day, and it listed the cause of death as "Sudden Unexplained Infant Death." I felt that dizzying trip-of-time sensation all day—where colors seemed too bright, noises seemed too loud, and everything seemed too alive. There hadn't been any question in my mind that SIDS was the cause, and from what I'd learned, SIDS and SUID were basically the same thing. The difference most likely was that she made it to the hospital rather than being pronounced dead at day care.

I cried when I opened the envelope. I wanted to read that the medical examiner was actually shocked to find that the doctors were the ones who screwed up, or maybe that Carla was at fault. I wanted a knock at the door and to find that the person on the other side was holding Isabelle. "Oops, there was a mistake," they'd say. "Here's your baby."

I continued to research SIDS and found dozens of reports that I wanted to keep. When the ink ran out of my printer, I travelled the quick mile to the real estate office to use their printers. My license and dues were paid up through the winter, and I figured I might as well get my money's worth. I'd seen the receptionist before. Her name was Deanna. She was tall, thin, and had short gray hair. My favorite thing about her was her friendly, grandmotherly smile. She manned the front desk in the evenings and she always seemed pleasant when I told her I was a visiting agent from another one of the company's real estate offices. This was the first time I'd been in to that office since before Isabelle's death and I didn't feel social. I tried to skitter past Deanna's desk to the resource room where the printers were, but when she said, "I know who you are," I stopped in my tracks.

Busted! I thought, and wondered how she could possibly know my devious plan to print papers that weren't related to real estate.

"Amy Lyon," I said and pulled one of my business cards out of my bag. "I'm an agent with the Lake Street office."

"I know all that," she said and waved her hand. "I work part time at the police department. I know about Isabelle."

Slap! My eyes must have looked like they were about to pop off my face, at least that's how I felt, because Deanna rose to her feet and reached out her hand.

"I'm so sorry," she said.

I shoved my hands into the pockets of my jeans and stared at her. How dare she say Isabelle's name? How dare she pretend to know what happened to my baby from reading a police report?

"She was a beautiful baby," she said and my body stiffened.

"How do you know?" I asked.

"There were pictures in her file," she said.

I knew the pictures Deanna referred to. They were taken by the police detective who came to the hospital. They were taken when Isabelle was motionless in the bed, hooked up to a dozen different tubes. I tried to walk away, but Deanna wasn't finished with me. She had questions. She asked how I was doing and how Chad was doing, and I found the grace to give her one- and two-word answers.

"I just don't get the whole SIDS thing," she said and my shoulders relaxed a little. I was just as mystified by SIDS as the next gal and it was nice to hear someone else say it out loud. "Did they find anything in the autopsy report?"

I shook my head as two other agents gathered around the front desk, apparently thinking Deanna was dishing good gossip.

"I just don't know how it could be called SIDS if Isabelle was awake and crying," she said, then looked to the other agents. "Amy's daughter, Isabelle, passed away recently at day care."

"What?" I spat. "I didn't know Isabelle was crying."

"Oh. yeah," Deanna said. "The report said she'd been crying and the day care lady found her on her stomach."

"Her stomach!" I shouted and fumbled for my keys.

Deanna's eyes twinkled and she nodded her head double-time. "We just lost another one, too," she said to one of the hovering agents.

"An agent?" the middle-aged man asked.

"No, another baby," Deanna said.

I huffed. For one of the first times in my life, I couldn't find my words.

"Yep. A baby from New Prague," Deanna rattled on. "A neighbor was babysitting the baby girl and they think it's SIDS, but it sounds more like the dad had something to do with it. It all seems very suspicious."

My fingers finally locked around the cold metal of my car keys and I yanked them from my bag. "What do you do at the police department?" I asked.

"Oh, I'm the receptionist," she said, and I just about tossed my cookies.

I rushed home, relayed the whole story to Chad, and found myself whirling through a tornado of emotions. *Why was Isabelle crying? Had one of the kids hurt her? Did Carla's cat get into the room and smother her? Was she put to sleep on her stomach when I specifically told Carla to put her to sleep on her back? Why was she crying?*

Chad took the next morning off of work and we stormed into the police station. Deanna wasn't at the front desk, but the receptionist who was there quickly summoned the detective who had questioned us at the hospital. When we briefly relayed the situation, she agreed to run off a copy of the police report. I asked her why we hadn't automatically gotten a copy of the report, and she said it wasn't standard procedure to pass along that information.

"The department's trying to save money," she said, and I noticed that her eyes weren't as kind as they were the day she came to the hospital. Still, she walked us through the lengthy report, which listed verbatim the phone call Carla had made to the police department and the questions she was asked by detectives. Carla had told the detectives that Isabelle had been crying, then stopped, and Carla went to check on her as soon as she finished making lunch for the other kids. I learned that the detective had found a small drop of blood on the crib sheet that she suspected had come from Isabelle's nose. A doctor had told her that sometimes when a heart stopped suddenly, it caused bleeding from the nose.

"Why weren't we told about this?" I asked.

"We didn't think it was important," she said.

I huffed. "Every detail is important. This is my daughter we're talking about."

"We didn't think it was important *to the case*," she clarified.

When she asked if we wanted to discuss anything else I launched into a rant about Deanna, her inappropriate comments, and how our private tragedy—and the tragedy of another couple—was broadcast by one of their employees. The detective called in Deanna's boss, who took a written statement.

"I find this hard to believe," he said. "Deanna's such a sweet grandmotherly-type. Everyone absolutely adores her here."

"So?" I said, feeling like I was the one who'd done something wrong by tattling on an innocent old lady. "She's also a gossip and likes to rummage through files that she really has no business looking through."

The man found his serious side and said that he would discuss the matter with human resources and determine the best action to take.

"This is a very serious situation," he assured me, and promised to call within the week to let me know of their decision with regards to Deanna. "I want to assure you that the situation will be taken care of."

A week came and went, one month turned into two, and he never called.

Chapter Thirteen

Chad needed something. He told me one night that he thought it might help to talk to people who had experienced what we were experiencing: a loss without words. When I found a listing in the local newspaper's community calendar for an infant loss support group, we went. The meeting was scheduled to take place at St. Francis Hospital, the same hospital where we delivered Isabelle. We arrived right at 7 p.m., waited for twenty minutes, but no one showed up.

"Talk about discouraging," Chad muttered as we sat in the back of the dimly lit chapel, facing each other. If we'd felt alone on this planet before, we'd now been catapulted into our own solar system.

Just as we stood to leave, a woman wandered in, surprised to see us there. Her name was Angela and she said she was the coordinator for the infant loss support group. While there were no other attendees, she offered her ear and we spilled our guts. Chad and I talked alternately for an hour-and-a-half about our struggles, our feelings, and the overwhelming pain we felt on a daily basis.

"It doesn't seem fair that bad things always seem to happen to good people," Angela said, and tears of genuine sympathy made her blue eyes sparkle.

I told her how conflicted I felt about bringing Isabelle to day care that Monday.

"God was ready to bring her home but didn't want you to be there," she said gently, but with that uncanny belief in a higher power that mystified me. "He knows what he's doing."

I winced. Maybe God did know what he was doing, but I felt it was high time he let the rest of us in on his big secret. I wanted to believe Angela, but I remained skeptical. God still had a lot of explaining to do.

On the drive home, Chad said he wondered if babies like Isabelle stopped breathing because they weren't totally developed and their brains just plain forgot.

"We think nine months incubating in mom is long enough, but maybe for some babies, despite their full grown size, there are still important things like that that need a little more time," he said.

"Maybe," I said. "And maybe that's why the incidents of SIDS pretty much drop off to nothing after the first year."

We were quiet for a while.

"Maybe it's kind of like the baby sea turtles," I said, remembering the Sea Turtle Hospital we toured in Marathon Key.

"Maybe," Chad said. "They just forget to breathe."

* * *

There was a peace within me the next day, a calm sensation that I'd felt in short blips on and off over the last week. On this day, though, the feeling was so overwhelming in intensity that if I were to measure it on an emotion scale, the reading would register as the complete opposite of pain. I wandered the yard with Raven, my fingertips resting on her head. She walked close to me, her black fur tickling my right leg. I shook my head, wondering where the feeling was coming from and if, by any chance, it was actually me detaching from my body and losing my mind. Raven and I stood in the area of the backyard that would soon be tilled, planted, and mulched to create Isabelle's Memorial Garden. I moved to the spot between two lilac trees where an arch of leaves formed over my head, and I felt the cool breeze and a nip of fall in the air.

"This has got to be God's doing," I whispered, wanting to believe, needing to believe. "I've never felt anything like this before."

Years later, still mystified by the feelings, I would reason that losing Isabelle hit me so hard that it cracked me wide open, exposing the very core of me, leaving a gaping hole that made me susceptible to bad and good, evil and grace. I became convinced it was God who immediately swooped in to fill the hole so as not to let evil take control. In addition to the worst kind of sadness, I was now programmed to feel the best kind of happiness.

I sat down in the grass and it was still there. That peace within me. And after losing Isabelle? How was it possible I felt Hope rising to her feet? How had she regained her strength after her clear defeat by Fear in the hospital? The cool breeze blew again and I closed my eyes, inviting the peaceful sensation to swirl around me. I felt it with every cell in my body. There was only one way to describe it. I felt God in the air.

* * *

Everyone knew I'd had a baby. Past coworkers, high school acquaintances, and those I ran into on an occasional basis. It's the kind of news you share with people because good news is hard to come by and, chances are, if you are pregnant with a baby, you will likely give birth to that baby and that baby will grow up. The questions pummeled me from every direction, "Did you have a boy or a girl?" "Where is the little tyke?" "Have you gone back to work?" And when I delivered the worst news a parent could hear—"Actually," I'd say, "Isabelle passed away."—the color would drain from their faces instantly.

Somehow I got used to delivering the line and answering follow-up questions, and after awhile I was able to swaddle my pain with the trust that Isabelle was safe in Heaven, and that kept the tears from falling.

One of the people who knew about our loss was my manager at the real estate office, Kyle Manson. He was a tall man with a gray hairpiece that I think he knew everyone else knew wasn't his real hair. Still, he was handsome, a "snappy dresser" as Grandpa would have called him. I often looked to Kyle during my four years in real estate as a mentor and, on occasion, a father figure. He had nearly 150 real estate agents to keep track of, and despite his busy schedule, he didn't just ask for updates about my clients and my open houses, he asked about Chad and seemed genuinely interested in my life outside of real estate. He joked with me and I appreciated his quick wit. He told me I was "a smart one" and even commented now and then on the articles I wrote for the local newspaper.

When my coworker, Pete, gave him the news that Isabelle was in the hospital, Pete said Kyle "got choked up" and "nearly broke down" in front of all the agents during the Tuesday morning business meeting. He came to the funeral and hugged me hard. Even in my despair, I was proud to introduce him to my own dad. So, when I scheduled time with Kyle on a Friday afternoon in mid-September to announce that I would leave real estate and spend the next year working on an advanced baby monitor, I was surprised that he was short on words.

"Sure, I understand," Kyle said from across his desk. His expression was blank and his hands were folded in front of him, resting on top of a large monthly calendar.

I guessed my news was the last thing he wanted to hear since the housing market was beginning a downward spiral into the toilet. Still, quitting was something I had to do, and I found myself slipping into the persona I prided myself on avoiding. I rationalized my decision to him. I explained and re-explained what I would do and why. I became desperate for his approval.

"The more research I do, the more I see a need for a baby monitor of some sort either to detect lack of movement, lack of breathing, or both," I said.

Kyle nodded and glanced at the clock, and I took my cue. We wrapped up our conversation when he suggested I go on the referral network until my license expired. That way, if I got any residual calls from clients, I could refer them on to Pete or another agent and still get a small commission.

All business, I thought, sadly, as I left the building and walked to my car. *Not even a "How are you and Chad doing?" or "You look good, considering…"* I questioned my decision on the drive home. I would be cutting our income by at least $40,000 per year, and although I planned to continue freelance writing from home and would sell my melted glass from the Web site, Chad and I would need to make major financial adjustments.

I ventured to tell a few people about the baby monitor and my uncertainty about the next year. No one questioned me. I wondered if they truly supported my decision or if they thought I was fragile, weak, and might crack in half if they expressed an opinion different from my own. I wasn't a baby and I wasn't a weakling, and I hoped no one saw me that way. But more than that, I hoped my plans for a baby monitor would progress to the point where, by the end of the next summer, when I looked back to assess my progress, I would realize there was no need to look back. *Clearly I did the right thing,* I would think. *Just look at what I've accomplished.*

When I arrived home that afternoon, I got to work. I composed a letter to our pediatrician thanking her for the care she gave Isabelle.

I told her about our four days at Children's Hospital, the discussions Chad had with Nurse Chris, and how I believed the number one fear among new parents is that their child will stop breathing.

"I wonder why there aren't 'advanced baby monitors' available that might also alert a parent if an infant's breathing stops," I wrote in the letter. "Nurse Chris explained that there are doctor-prescribed apnea monitors, which infants must be approved for, but nothing that is available to the general public that is also easily portable (to take to grandma's house or day care)."

I told her that in my research I'd also learned that home monitoring systems to detect a lack of movement had not been well received by the medical community.

Dr. Philip responded two days later via e-mail. She said that since Isabelle's death, she had made an increased effort to stress SIDS education for parents, not only at the newborn period, but continually reminding them at infant well checks. She also said she spoke with several of her colleagues to get their feedback on an advanced baby monitor, and found that most physicians were comfortable with the medically-advised apnea monitors because of the follow-up and feedback received from it.

"The main point from this is that you need a monitor that can be reliable enough to go off when it needs to, but not be so sensitive it unnecessarily alarms parents and care providers," Dr. Philip wrote. "This may lead to many children being hospitalized overnight for possible 'apnea' episodes, or parents/caregivers ignoring it because of so many false alarms. The monitor itself is not foolproof, and can often go off unexpectedly because the probes become disconnected, or baby is moving, kicking, or the calibration of the equipment is off. It tends to be quite sensitive."

Their main concern with a home monitor like I wanted to create was that a parent could become too reliant on it and substitute it for frequent parental checks, and one doctor mentioned cases of SIDS that occurred despite monitoring.

"I do not want to discourage you from finding ways to prevent SIDS and educate parents, but these seem to be the biggest concerns regarding home monitoring," she wrote. "I truly hope that research in the field of SIDS does find some answers that would help us all. I know I am a pediatrician, but I am a mother above all, and anything that would reduce infant death would be worth its money."

I sighed heavily when I finished reading her letter, a mixture of encouragement and frustration. I appreciated Dr. Philip's honesty, but I felt like she sort of missed the point. Or maybe I secretly longed for a hip-hip-hooray from her. I knew my limitations. I wasn't trying to cure SIDS. I would leave that to the experts, but until those experts could figure out the cause, there needed to be something that could, at the very least, alert parents if a baby rolled onto its stomach, a sleeping position that was frowned upon by the American Academy of Pediatrics.

I tried not to let the medical community's concerns of home monitoring deter me, even though they were doctors and I was, well, not a doctor. I continued to research the subject and then found myself acting on an unfamiliar impulse. I put my hands together. "Dear God, should I be doing this? Can I do this? Create a baby monitor?" I shook my head. "I'm gonna need your help."

* * *

The first biting chill of fall swirled in the end of September air, and though the week had been windy and cold, the temperature was warm and the sky was cloudless on the Saturday we created Isabelle's Memorial Garden. Chad had kept in touch with Carla and learned that her husband owned a landscaping business. When he heard about the transformation that was to take place in our backyard, he offered his help to design the layout. He also gave us a discount on dirt fill and mulch, and by noon on Saturday our yard was bustling with family members and friends dressed in work clothes, toting shovels and carrying plant off-shoots from their own gardens.

Chad's mom brought a small angel statue that made Chad cry and my mom sent money to have a rock engraved with the words, "Isabelle's Garden." Mom and Kim also purchased a brown bench and accompanying cushions that was placed between the two lilac trees. Kim had a nameplate engraved with the words, "In Loving Memory of Isabelle."

I brimmed with gratefulness that day. Chad's mom said I "glowed," and it seemed there would be no end to the memorial garden offerings. Chad's dad showed up with a magnolia tree. Chad's sister, Jennie, brought forget-me-not flowers. His other sister, Andre, unveiled concrete stepping stones made by Isabelle's cousins, Nick and Lexy, that said "Isabelle, My Angel Cousin" and "Isabelle, Forever In My Heart."

I took pictures throughout the day, and that night created a Web site that showed the transformation from beginning to end with all of the work in between. The rectangular-shaped flower garden was flanked on the left corners by a pink-flowering apple blossom tree given to us by the parents at Carla's day care, and, just behind it, the magnolia. Because the left side received the most sunlight, we planted light-loving plants such as purple coneflowers, black-eyed Susans, Shasta daisies, and other assorted perennials whose names I had yet to learn. The opposite side of the garden was anchored by the two lilac trees with the bench snuggled in between, sheltered under the trees' low branches and, at the beginning of each spring, fragrant dark purple flowers.

Chad and I hung two wind chimes above the bench. My wind chime was made of glass and metal and offered sweet, high tinkling sounds, while Chad's wind chime was made of bamboo and made a low, hollow sound that soothed me in the pit of my stomach. At the back of the garden, we placed a concrete, daisy-shaped birdbath that I'd painted with a yellow center, off-white leaves, and green pedestal stem. Shade-loving hostas and lilies bordered an unmarked walkway that circled around a 30-foot-tall ash tree in the center. In front of that ash tree we created a raised bed where we placed the angel statue and the "Isabelle's Garden" rock, as well as a few pots and planters I'd picked up at a thrift store. I planned to fill the pots with annuals, such as Gerber daisies and petunias.

I finished off the Web site by adding photos down the left column of Isabelle, interspersed with some of my favorite inspirational sayings and poems: "Perhaps they are not stars in the sky, but rather openings where our loved ones shine down to let us know they are happy"; "The decision to become a mother, it's momentous. It is to decide forever to have your heart go walking around outside your body"; and my favorite, "I shall think of her as smiling, for what else would one do in the presence of God?" At the bottom of the page I added a photo of Isabelle by the lake during our trip to the art fair, as well as the treasured "Gone From My Sight" poem by Henry Van Dyke that Mom had given me. After I uploaded the Web site to the Internet, Chad and I sat together on the bench in Isabelle's Garden.

"Can you believe this?" I asked as I leaned into him. "The work done in one day would have easily taken us a month or two."

"At least," Chad agreed.

I began to cry and Chad hugged me tight. Then I felt his stomach quiver under my arm and I knew he was crying, too.

* * *

I went to the real estate office one afternoon during the next week to drop off the "status change" paperwork that would strip me of my full-time real estate agent status. While there, I wound up divulging my plans for a baby monitor to another agent named Andy. I didn't have a close relationship with him, but I felt compelled to share my plans with him. My instincts were right, because he gave me the contact information for a woman named Cynthia Schroeder, who worked as one of the directors at the University of Minnesota Medical Foundation in Minneapolis.

I contacted Cynthia and two days later we had lunch at Sally's, a trendy little restaurant on the University campus.

"First and foremost you need to have a prototype created," Cynthia said as she bit into her sandwich. She then suggested I contact the University engineering department to talk to a teacher about the possibility of making the creation of the advanced baby monitor a class assignment.

"You also shouldn't rule out the idea of going to a company like Medtronic," she said, speaking of the well-known Minneapolis-based leader in the creation of medical technologies.

We finished our lunch, collected our things, and on the way out the door she stopped and touched my arm. "I just want you to know that I know you're going to make this happen. You seem like the type of person who gets things done."

Chapter Fourteen

At the beginning of October, I found myself pacing in front of the refrigerator calendar, counting and recounting the days of my monthly cycle. I was five days late and, knowing that my reproductive system was incredibly prompt, I was pretty sure I was pregnant.

Chad and I had talked extensively about having another baby while we were in the Keys and I even sat down one afternoon on the beach and prayed out loud to both God and Isabelle: "I want to have another baby, God. Isabelle, you must known I would never try to replace you. If this isn't the right time, please let me know somehow."

In flipping through the pages of the grief books, my eyes landed on a paragraph about future pregnancies. It said that a woman's body needed time to heal and that another pregnancy within the first year likely would not allow a person to grieve properly. I worried that other people would think it was too soon. Would they think I didn't feel sad about Isabelle anymore? Would they think I'd moved on?

I took a pregnancy test that night and it registered negative. I knew it was wrong so I waited patiently for an hour and took another test. Still negative. I took another pregnancy test two days later and it came back positive, a blurry positive, but positive nonetheless. I immediately thanked God and rubbed my belly. God and Isabelle approved and I was elated. Chad was at his friend Joe's house, and I took a picture of the pregnancy test with my phone and messaged it to Chad. I immediately got a picture message back of his smiling face, and he looked like a midget compared to Joe's six-foot-five frame in the background.

"You told Joe!" I hollered seconds later when I called Chad. I tried to sound angry, but joy danced atop every word I spoke. "I don't want anyone to know!"

"Okay," Chad said, and I could hear the happiness in his voice, too. "Joe won't tell anyone."

"I'm telling everyone!" Joe shouted in the background, then I heard a beep and a click and I knew Chad had put me on speakerphone.

"I don't want anyone to know!" I repeated, then said, "Chad take me off speakerphone now."

"Okay," he said, laughing. I loved hearing him laugh again.

"Really, I don't want anyone else to know. Even your family. At least for a while. I'm worried they'll think it's too soon."

"Who cares what they think?" Chad said.

"I know, I know. I just want to wait."

I hung up the phone, popped some popcorn, and turned on a Lifetime movie about a college professor who was having an affair with one of her students. I half-watched the drama unfold and rubbed the area that would soon swell with life. I'd lost most of my baby weight during the postpartum depression and, after Isabelle passed away, the remaining weight disappeared within two weeks. Now I looked forward to my skin stretching again and the ripple-ripple of baby kicks.

* * *

I felt good on Sundays after I went to church, which still surprised me, so I signed up for a weekend Women's Church Retreat with pastoral intern Linda McPeak. I'd first met Linda the day after Isabelle passed away. She came to our house and to the funeral home with Pastor Tom. I wasn't a church retreat kind of gal, but what drew me in to the whole deal was Linda and the location. I wasn't about to commit to an overnight getaway, but the way Linda organized the retreat allowed me to go home to my own bed each night and, if for some reason the whole deal was too much for me, I could leave and be home within ten minutes. I wasn't trapped.

Friday night involved a casual gathering at a church member's beautiful home overlooking Prior Lake. I'd always been comfortable showing up at events where I didn't know anyone and I was glad to see that this event was no exception. There was a glimmer of my old self, a part that I liked, that was still hidden in there underneath all of the pain. The ladies were dressed casually, jeans mostly, and we socialized and some people drank wine. I snacked on strawberries dipped in a fondue fountain of chocolate. When I thought no one was looking, I swiped my finger through the stream and lapped up the rich sugary goodness. Clearly Baby Lyon had a sweet tooth.

The subject of the retreat was "Finding Your Joy," and Linda was prepared with discussion topics and worksheets. I liked structure, so the layout of the event suited me well. The first worksheet asked the question, "What would you do if you knew you could not fail?" My pencil hit the light green paper as soon as the words registered and I scribbled, "Create the Izzy Bell Advanced Baby Monitor, bring the product to the market, and tour the country educating about SIDS."

My pencil stopped but my thoughts continued. *I would teach everyone to put their babies to sleep on their backs without blankets or stuffed animals in the cribs. I would create a foundation that would raise money to make the baby monitor available to low-income individuals who couldn't afford it.*

We went around the room and read our answers out loud. Linda started with the woman next to me, so that I was the last person to speak. She winked at me with kind eyes and I wondered if she had planned it that way. One woman said she would quit her job as an administrative assistant to be a party planner if she could not fail. I smiled and wished she would try it. Another woman simply wanted to balance her time better between family and work, and another woman wanted to go back to school. When it was my turn, I read my answer out loud and explained the reasoning behind it. There was a collective gasp in the room.

"This was only two months ago?" one woman asked, and she quickly crossed the room to hug me. She wiped away her tears and I told her to stop crying so I wouldn't cry. It was a habit now and I hated that I always told people to stop crying on my account. Why stop? Why not let the whole room break down in tears? Why couldn't I just let people be sad for me?

We took a break for more food and drinks, and Linda scooted onto the chair next to me. She had a nice, simple haircut that made her thick brown strands curl under politely. She wore khaki shorts, a T-shirt, and brown sandals. I liked that she didn't pull out the frills and wear a church gown or something. She was one of us. Not better. Not worse.

"I'm really glad you came," she said and touched my leg. I felt the warmth of her hand through my jeans. "How are you doing?"

Linda asking the question was different from the way most people asked it. She was genuine to her core and she really wanted to know, I thought, and so I spilled. After I shared how much I missed Isabelle every single minute of every single day, I told her about my plans for the Izzy Bell Advanced Baby Monitor and expressed my frustration with not knowing how to create a prototype.

"I'm not an engineer," I said. "I read a book about provisional patents and I think I understand that, but I wouldn't even know how to go about creating a prototype. I just feel so strongly about this—"

She laughed a little and I said, "I know, I know, I get all wound up. I need to settle down."

Linda shook her head. "No, it's not that. My husband is an engineer for a medical device company."

My mouth fell open. "Really?"

Linda told me about the local company, Devicix, that Tom McPeak and four other engineers had started three years earlier. She said that the partners had always dreamed of finding a product from an inventor and working with that inventor from start to finish.

That night when I got home, I pulled up the company's Web site and started to cry.

"Chad!" I yelled and relayed to him the discussion I'd had with Linda, then showed him the Web site. "It seems like such a perfect fit."

Chad nodded. "Wow," he said. He joked that he had the idea in the hospital and the rest was up to me.

"Remember," I said. "An idea is nothing without proper execution."

Chad rolled his eyes and rubbed my back.

I scrolled through the Devicix Web site with an anxiousness stirring in my belly. I had no idea how this baby monitor was going to come to life, but I felt confident I could make it work.

Saturday's portion of the church retreat included a full day of discussing dreams, goals for the future, and roadblocks. The other ladies talked about how they tried to give up their worries to God and asked him for signs of where to go next. I thought they were a little over the top, but then I tried *giving up my worries* during a meditative prayer session Linda led. *God,* I thought, and I paused a long while before going on. Was this seriously going to work? *If you think the baby monitor is a good idea, I have the passion and energy to move it forward. I just need your help.* Then I added, *and your guidance,* because I'd heard one of the other women use that phrase.

I felt energized that evening when I went home and shuffled mulch around in Isabelle's Garden before I collapsed on the bench, exhausted. Baby Lyon took a lot out of me. As I sat in the garden I searched for butterflies like the one that had landed on my leg, but there were none. I looked for a bird to swoop down in front of my face, but that didn't happen. The wind chimes tinkled high and thumped low, but it was their usual music. There was nothing out of the ordinary. I expected a sign from God, but, as usual, he didn't deliver…not on that day—and not as I expected, at least.

The next day, Sunday, the same eleven women met in the afternoon at the church for lunch and a prayer session. Linda had moved a few pews to the front of the church, around the baptismal bowl, which was filled with water. She gave us each a smooth, black rock.

"Let's take a few minutes and put our thoughts, worries, prayers, and questions to God into this rock," she said. "Then, when you're ready, slip the rock into the baptismal bowl, releasing those thoughts and worries to God."

I looked around at the other women's faces. They all had their eyes closed, shiny black rocks tucked safely into their folded hands. I felt angry for some reason. Angry at God again. It occurred to me to hurl the rock across the chapel and stomp out of the church, and I figured that might have been acceptable considering my circumstances. I stayed put, though, until the words finally formed, lifted, and swirled in my mind.

God, this is just too hard. I'm sure it was you who sent the grandma bird to the hospital and the butterfly that landed on my leg, but I need more than that. Those things could easily have been coincidences. I need something concrete, proof that Isabelle is okay. I don't know if that's even something you do, but that's what I need from you.

A few women had finished, and I stood up, walked to the bowl, squeezed the rock as hard as I could with my left hand and added, *Please God, this is what I need,* before I released it into the water.

I e-mailed Linda Sunday night and thanked her for the retreat. I also mentioned that I was very interested in meeting with her husband to tell him about the baby monitor. I realized that if a company performed a service, like creating a prototype, they needed to be paid for that service, but I tried not to focus on the money. I'd hold a fundraiser dinner with a dance afterward, or I'd increase the equity line on our house, if that was even possible. As constantly consumed as I was about our finances, the money didn't matter to me. I remembered the saying, *When one door closes, another door opens*, and I believed I heard creaking.

* * *

Two days later, I received a frantic call from Chad. He'd left work early and he was crying. It was the kind of phone call that now stopped my heart.

"I just had lunch with Andre," he said, his voice crackling.

"Is she okay?" I asked, surprised. Usually lunch with his sister made him feel better, not worse. Andre's family had spent a lot of time with Isabelle during her four months of life, frequently inviting her over to play, and Andre openly talked about the things she missed most about our baby, her niece. Maybe she'd said something that made Chad sad.

"Andre had a dream Sunday night," he said, "that she was in the hospital with Isabelle."

I pressed the phone to my ear, straining to hear Chad through the pounding of my heart.

"She was holding Isabelle like she had in the hospital, saying things like 'Please don't go,' and 'We need you here,' and Isabelle opened her eyes and said, 'Andre! I'm OK. I'm in Heaven and I don't hurt anymore.'"

I gasped. "She was talking?"

"No, Andre said her little brown eyes were open and she could hear the soft voice, but Isabelle's lips weren't moving. And then—" Chad practically choked on his words, "—and then Isabelle said she was okay and… 'There's another one on the way.'"

My vision blurred and the room spun around me…or maybe I spun around it. "What? She said that? How did she know that? You're kidding me!"

There's another one on the way.

"No, I'm not," Chad said, and underneath all of that pain I could hear hope in his voice. "And I started crying and Andre felt bad for telling me so she started crying. She said she called mom when she woke up, because she didn't know if she should tell us about it or not. She worried that we'd think she was pressuring us to have another baby."

"So, did you tell her?" I asked.

"I had to," Chad said.

"I know. You had to. I can't believe she had that dream. How could she have known we were pregnant?"

Chad was quiet for a few seconds. "Well, she didn't know," Chad said. "Isabelle told her."

I slipped to the floor and wept. *Isabelle told her.* Chad told me Andre initially thought Isabelle was talking about the assembly line of babies she imagined God had in Heaven, and that another baby was already picked out for us, "on its way," whenever we were ready. *Isabelle told her.*

"I told her, 'Andre, we *are* pregnant,'" Chad said and Andre started crying, too, then yelped with excitement.

"That's amazing," I said, and remembered the rock I'd released Sunday afternoon and the request I'd made to God. *I need something concrete, proof that Isabelle is okay...I don't know if that's even something you do, but that's what I need.*

Andre's dream had come that night.

The rest of the day I was buoyed by my belief and later that night we gathered with Chad's family for Buck Burger Night at the American Legion, where I officially shared our news with everyone. Thankfully, no one said, "You're pregnant? Already?" Instead, there were tears and smiles and hugs, and then Andre shared her dream with the group. Andre had always been open about wanting us to have a baby and she treated Isabelle like one of her own. Sometimes she called herself "Mommy" on accident when she held Isabelle, then jumped, apologized, and giggled. I didn't mind. At that time, I'd needed all the help I could get.

"I figured my dream just meant that whenever you guys are ready, Isabelle wants you to know she's okay with you having another baby," Andre told me that night, and I shared with her the prayer request I'd made on Sunday.

"Your dream makes me believe Isabelle really is okay in Heaven," I said through teary eyes, "and that she and God are okay with us having another baby. That it's the right time." I looked down at my lap, then up at Andre. "You have no idea how much this means to me."

Andre nodded and stared off into the distance. "It was just the clearest dream I've ever had, and it was so nice to see Isabelle again."

* * *

Chad and I received a letter from the Minnesota SID Center at Children's Hospital in Minneapolis that told us about a monthly SIDS support group, which turned out to be the next evening. We decided to go. As Chad's red truck bounced over the speed bumps into the parking ramp of the hospital, I felt a torturous knot in my stomach. My breathing sped up. We were back at the place that had caused us so much pain only a few months earlier. That wasn't the intention of the organizers, I was sure. Most babies didn't make it to the hospital in circumstances like ours. They were *pronounced* at the scene. I started to think of Isabelle as our little fighter. She tried so hard to stay with us, to hold on like we'd asked of her.

We walked along the skyway system that attached the parking ramp to the hospital building. I'd walked the same skyway a few times during our four days there, when the other areas of the building became too repetitive and I desperately needed a change of scenery. I reached for Chad's hand and we leaned into each other, ambling forward.

Maybe this isn't such a good idea, I thought as my body seemed to curl and twist inside itself to try to find comfort. We followed a sign that led us past a life-size figure of Big Bird and several playful, colorful sculptures designed to entertain and bring comfort to kids. The room we were directed to was across from the chapel where my sister had prayed and I had listened.

There was one other couple in the room, a woman our age, and an older woman who introduced herself as Shirley, the group's moderator. Another couple entered as we sat down. Despite the uncomfortably familiar atmosphere of the hospital, I did feel relieved to be in the company of others who might have some clue as to how we felt. I still felt alone, though. Others entered, and two girls whispered back and forth and even laughed once.

Someone mentioned that the group was a small one that night, and although a desperate part of me wanted a roomful of people, a tiny, gracious part of me wanted an empty room. The more people, the more pain. And I didn't want anyone else to feel what I felt.

When Shirley sat down, the room became quiet, and the silence and fluorescent light bulbs buzzed in my ears. Shirley had short, gray hair and a friendly demeanor. She was soft-spoken as she went through "the ground rules for the group." She told us, "This is one place where it is okay to cry." Then she instructed us each to go around the room, say our name and our baby's name, then the date of birth and the date of death. The contents of my stomach, a Dairy Queen cookie-dough Blizzard, moved to my throat and I reached for Chad's hand. I knew he wouldn't be able to say the words, so I would be the strong one. I would introduce us.

The first woman's baby died three years before, the second couple's died two years before, and the third a year before, then all eyes turned to us.

"I'm Amy and this is Chad," I said, successfully. "Our baby—" my voice cracked and my tear ducts, dry for almost a day, sprang a leak. I leaned into Chad and through blurry eyes I saw someone push the box of tissues toward me. I dared to look around and saw one of the other moms crying too. I looked to Chad.

"Our daughter, Isabelle, was born on March 27 and passed away on July 26," Chad said, and his voice cracked and then he started to cry.

I clutched a sopping-wet tissue in my right hand. "It's still very fresh," I said as if I had to explain.

The girl across from me started to cry and she nodded. We told our story of losing Isabelle in that very building and how we felt so alone in our grieving. Then the other women in the room spoke in turns, and it was like they plucked the words right off my tongue. A favor, it felt like, so I wouldn't have to speak. The moms spoke about the ignorance of friends and family members, how others made comments that turned out to be more hurtful than helpful, and how their arms ached to hold their babies. They spoke about the loneliness they felt until they'd found the people in that room who knew better than anyone, even the doctors, how it felt to have…and then to have not.

One dad said it was hard to be considered "the protector" of a family and offered that he felt like he'd completely failed as a husband and a father after his son died. Out of my peripheral vision I saw Chad's head nod several times, then he spoke.

"I'm worried I'll never feel better," Chad said, and no one discounted his feelings. I liked that. Instead, one dad recounted his own fears at the beginning of his "grief journey," and talked about the changes that had occurred in him since then. Maybe his words would give Chad hope. I hoped so.

No one gave us guarantees of happy days ahead, and I appreciated that honesty the most. I'd heard enough empty promises from armchair optimists professing that I "would feel better someday" or that I "wouldn't always feel this bad." Instead, here was a group of parents who'd been to the same hell as me and came out of it for another crack at life. They were the ones I wanted to hear from.

Near the end of the meeting, the conversation turned to subsequent pregnancies after losing a baby to SIDS, and I felt like my month-old baby bump had suddenly morphed to full term. I was ashamed.

"It's not unusual for a woman to be pregnant in this group," Shirley said, and her gentle eyes stopped briefly on each of us. I felt like her eyes lingered on me and I had to look away. I felt guilty. Guilty of being over it. Guilty of being pregnant too soon. Guilty of trying to replace Isabelle. All things I worried other people would think of me.

"And it's okay to talk about how hard it is to see pregnant women," Shirley continued. "Expectant mothers won't be offended. Most likely they've felt that way, too."

One of the women talked about how she hid her pregnancy from that very group under giant sweatshirts and sweaters. Like me, she worried other people might think it was too soon to bring another baby into the world, that people might think she was "over" her daughter that had died. I knew exactly what she meant. I often felt guilty for thinking about the new baby and feeling excited about him or her, as if I was forgetting about Isabelle. Then, a second later I felt guilty for neglecting the new baby by thinking only of Isabelle. And the cycle continued round and round.

Chad reached over and squeezed my hand. It seemed like the woman, the one who'd worn the big sweatshirts, talked directly to me, as if there were a giant spotlight on me and someone in the background screaming, "Guilty! This one's guilty of getting pregnant too soon!"

My face flushed, and again I had to look away, just as Shirley announced the close of our meeting. I was excited about the new baby, but it wouldn't be until the end of my pregnancy and nearly nine months of support group meetings that I would truly accept this baby as a gift from God and Isabelle. In fact, it would be in that support group that I would meet some of the most important people in my life—mothers and fathers who dared to share their heart-wrenching stories. Their presence in my life would obliterate the loneliness Chad and I had felt in our grief. Mothers would talk about subsequent pregnancies, their "rainbow babies," and, through the sharing of their gut-level feelings, I would learn that nearly every thought I'd had related to losing Isabelle at least one other mother had had, too.

Chapter Fifteen

In the guide, "Starting a Business in Minnesota," it is suggested that serious business people consider incorporating their business. So, the second week in December, Chad and I met with two separate attorneys in downtown Minneapolis to discuss our options. Chad's mom worked as a paralegal at a three-name law firm, so she connected us with one of the attorneys she knew. I'm no expert in legal consultation, but my time in real estate taught me the importance of the initial contact with a potential client. This lawyer was completely unprepared for our arrival and, although I knew we were mere minnows, he really did make us feel like small fish in a big pond.

The second lawyer we contacted was recommended to me by a coworker at the real estate office. The coworker's dad, who owned successful wine shops in the Twin Cities, used this attorney for every legal aspect of his business. Barbara Lano Rummel had been an attorney for seventeen years, and from the coffee she offered us to the enormous conference room she'd reserved for our meeting, I felt like she took us as seriously as if we were Warren Buffet or Donald Trump. She was middle-aged with lawyerly short blonde hair, of average height and average features, but she made me feel above average when she asked questions about our "product." She took notes with an expensive-looking pen on a yellow legal pad and nodded intently, her head tipped slightly to the right as she listened. She was also prepared with a list of questions she thought we should answer for ourselves about the business we planned to start. The questions ranged from "What are your goals and motivating factors?" to "Where do you hope to see the business in one, five, and ten years?" There was also a question that asked how we planned to raise the capital we needed for our company.

Capital? I thought. *That must mean money.*

"Of course I'm not going to charge you for this session," Barbara said at the end of one hour. "I'd love nothing more than to see your company succeed and to be a part of that success."

Sure, it sounded like a line, but I bit. Maybe she felt sorry for us because we'd lost Isabelle, but she didn't show us pity and I appreciated that. Or, maybe it was customary to offer a free session when trying to reel in a new client. Either way, her kindness propelled me forward and I felt like I was able to add another person to my corner.

Chad was quiet on the 26-floor elevator ride to the parking garage while I flipped through the information Barbara had given us. In the car, I read her bio, amazed at how perfect her background seemed for the Izzy Bell project.

"Listen to this," I said to Chad as he veered onto the exit out of downtown that would take us to our south suburban home. "Barb counsels public and privately held businesses—particularly medical device and biotechnology companies—in organizing new ventures and raising capital through public and private financing."

"Wow," Chad said.

"Oh, and get this. She also facilitates product development, and handles licensing and distribution arrangements."

I flipped to the list of questions she wanted us to answer and my eyes landed on the word *motivation.* "What is your motivation for starting this company?" I said out loud, but Chad didn't answer. Well, that was an easy one for me. I was motivated by my love for Isabelle. What better motivation could there be? I also felt motivated by the thousands of babies who die each year from SIDS. If I could save just one…well, that would be at least one less parent who had to feel the way I felt.

I needed to find a reason for Isabelle's death—even if I had to create that reason myself.

* * *

Just before Christmas, I met with Linda McPeak's husband, Tom, and the owner of Devicix, Pete. I relayed my baby monitor plan to them and Tom said, "It definitely sounds doable."

Pete explained that writing a business plan needed to be my first action step, followed by the creation of a prototype. I needed to have something tangible that I could show to potential investors that would hopefully propel them to invest in my idea. And, from his initial estimates, it seemed I would need quite a bit of money, not just for the prototype, but also for the first product run.

Pete offered to create a financial spreadsheet in Excel that I could use to help me determine a sales price for the baby monitor and estimate sales for the first five years. Tom offered to research devices, and the two engineers proceeded to use words like accelerometer, oscillator, and opto-mechanical tilt switch. When I got home that night, I Googled the words they used and read page after page about the devices until I had at least a basic understanding of how they worked.

Truthfully, I knew I was out of my league. There were people in my life who had hinted that I had no business trying to start a business, or to create a brand new product with my lack of experience, especially in my grieving, pregnant condition. But I felt propelled to move forward, sure that this had to be the direction in which God wanted me to go. What other explanation could there be for my sudden ability to understand the nuances of patent lingo and financial pro forma worksheets?

I asked Chad to sit down with me for a brainstorming session, but it seemed forced. He had ideas and thoughts now and then, but I could tell he wanted to leave the detail work to me. I was fine with that, or at least I said I was fine with that. We had agreed that I would quit real estate, freelance write for the newspaper from home to help pay the bills and spend the rest of my time working on the baby monitor. So that's what I would do.

Using an online trial membership for the James J. Hill reference library, I searched the next day and I found two 100-plus page reports that seemed like they'd come in handy: "The U.S. Market for Infant, Toddler and Preschool Home Furnishings and Accessories" and "The U.S. Moms Market Report." The reports contained the important factoids I would use to build the backbone of my business plan's marketing section.

I already knew from U.S. Census data I'd found on the Internet that approximately 4.1 million babies were born in the United States each year, a number that had steadily increased by about one percent each of the last twenty years. "The U.S. Moms Market Report" broke that number down among five age groups and I saw an obvious trend when I put the numbers into table format: 87 percent of babies were born to Generation X and Y parents, which I called my "target market."

From there, I researched the spending patterns and shopping preferences of my target market. Months later, as my business plan progressed, I would add licensed day care services as a secondary market, noting that census reports estimated 663,843 licensed day care establishments nationwide. I knew from personal experience that a day care center could benefit from the Izzy Bell Advanced Baby Monitor.

At the library the next day, I found a title that made my heart sing: *Household Spending: Who Spends How Much on What.* I carried the massive hardcover book to a table and flipped through the pages of endless data until I found a section on "Infant Equipment." There, my soul was nourished with tables of annual average spending on infant equipment by age, location, race, and income level. I used the data to create more tables in my business plan, which helped to break up the text and made the pages visually pleasing.

"Investors love tables and graphs and pie charts," Pete had told me during our meeting.

As the weeks went by, my research continued. The Internet, specifically Google, was my research ally. I found magazine articles, quoted them, and those quotes added a credibility that helped me build the muscle that strengthened my business plan. For example, one article highlighted the $2.6 billion dollars U.S. parents regularly spend on baby goods with a large chunk going to gadgets like monitors and thermometers. Another forecasted that kids' equipment sales would grow by 8.9 percent in the next five years. And with a quote from one of the reports, I further highlighted Generations X and Y's desire for technologically advanced products.

Later that day, laying on the living room floor and rubbing my belly, I found the golden nugget I'd been searching for. According to an article in *Forbes* magazine citing an international study, the most important baby gadget all over the world "was likely the baby monitor."

And with that, my business plan had a heart—and it was beating wildly!

I often shared with Chad in the evenings the "golden nuggets" I'd dug up during the day, and that night, I was beside myself with enthusiasm.

"You're sort of an idiot savant," he said over dinner. Spaghetti again.

I eyed him warily. "Is that your attempt at a compliment?"

I flipped open my laptop. "Dictionary.com," I said as I typed. "*Idiot savant.*" I read the definition. "A mentally defective person—"

"What!?" Chad said, then pushed back from the table and came to stand behind me. "...with an exceptional skill or talent," he said, holding his hands up in defense.

"Not a compliment," I muttered.

He pulled me to my feet. "Maybe you're just an idiot then," he said playfully and hugged me tight.

In the following weeks, the facets of my business plan flowed freely from my fingertips, and when I showed it to Pete at Devicix, he was floored.

"I can't believe you put this together yourself," he said, then showed the plan to several people in his office, highlighting some of his favorite parts. I blushed as he continued to read out loud, then gave him a copy to put in my file.

"You're ready," Pete said.

"Ready for what?" I asked.

"Ready to go hunt down investors," he said.

* * *

In mid-December, I set the business plan aside with plans to pick it up after the New Year. I'd learned how to create formulas in Excel from an online tutorial and had read a handful of dry how-to books in my effort to create an impressive picture for investors. I wasn't quite ready to take the next step in search of investors. I'd worked so intensely over the last two months that my frazzled brain needed a break. And as Christmas approached, I felt a stronger-than-usual desire to help people. So, when the opportunity to volunteer dressed as an elf at a local children's home appeared before me, I gleefully took it.

And as it turned out, the elf outing got me addicted to *doing good*. I sought out opportunities at Cross of Peace where I could volunteer, and I found that it was healing for me to focus my energy on helping others. I'd also found that the last days of months were especially difficult as I thought about Isabelle's birth date on the 27th and her Heaven date on the 26th. And with Christmas being only a few days away, my emotions were on high alert.

When Chad's family asked for our Christmas lists, it took everything in me not to shout, "We won't be celebrating this year or ever again!" In the end, I sent an e-mail to our families telling them we were having a hard time with the holidays and couldn't compile the lists they'd requested. Whatever they got us would be fine, I wrote. In later years, as the fog of grief lifted somewhat, I would ask that, in lieu of gifts, money could be donated in Isabelle's memory to a variety of charities.

I didn't get to know her much, but it felt like something Isabelle would want.

Chapter Sixteen

For Christmas, Chad's mom gave us a pewter ornament that made everyone in the house cry. The front of the ornament said, "I love you all dearly, now don't shed a tear, I'm spending my Christmas with Jesus this year." On the back were the engraved words, "Love Isabelle."

Chad gave me a Build-a-Bear Workshop gift card for Christmas, and on December 30, we went to the mall to build our Izzy Bear. A woman from our support group had given us the idea to build a bear and to dress her in an angel outfit to resemble Isabelle in our family photos.

"It reminds people that you have a child even if they don't see her like your other children," the woman had said during our December support group meeting.

The Build-a-Bear store was crazy busy with kids picking out special bears, stuffing them full, placing hearts inside, then doing the magic dance to bring their bears to life. Chad and I selected a white bear with a few sprigs of pink in the fur. We got in line, selected our heart, and each said a prayer and made wishes while clutching the little piece of red plastic. The heart was placed inside the bear with its "magical" stuffing.

"Okay, now jump up three times and spin around!" said the bear-stuffing employee dressed in an elf costume.

"No thanks," I said while the conflicting emotions of embarrassment and despair bounced around inside of me. "Just fill the bear please."

"It won't work unless you do it!" she insisted with a red-lipped smile.

I hopped limply a couple of times. "That's the best I can do," I said and pointed to my belly. "I'm pregnant."

Her grin grew wider. "Is this bear for your baby?" she asked as she pumped a peddle that sent white stuffing whirling around inside a clear, plastic compartment.

I looked to Chad, whose face was blank.

"No, our daughter passed away and we're creating this bear in remembrance of her," I said flatly.

The employee seemed unaffected as she grinned with glee and continued stuffing.

"Do you know if you have angel wings for the bear?" I asked.

The elf woman stitched the bear's back closed, then gently handed it to me. She hopped off her seat and shuffled to the back of the store, the bells on her hat jingling. She returned empty handed. "We had angel wings before Christmas, but we don't have any left." She tipped her head and made a frowny face. "I think you can still order them online."

Chad and I thanked her and shopped the store for an outfit for the Izzy Bear. We found a white, angelic-looking dress, but it came with a veil.

"This must be a wedding dress," Chad said. We looked at each other and knew without words that we'd never see our daughter off to her prom or watch her walk down the aisle in a wedding dress.

"We can make this work," I said determinedly and yanked the veil from the packaging. "They can keep this part. The dress is pretty, though." It was a sleeveless satin dress with a little poof to the skirt.

Chad found white shoes decorated with iridescent daisies and slipped them onto the bear's feet. We stood in line to pay and as we approached the register, we noticed several employees gathered around the cashier, looking at us.

"You were looking for the angel wings," one of them said. "I just looked online and they're still there."

"Thank you," I said.

"This is a beautiful bear," the cashier said and looked up at us. "It's a nice way to remember your daughter."

"Thank you," I said again.

The Izzy Bear was put into a cute little carrying box with a handle, and as we walked the hallway of the mall toward the exit, I opened the box just a little so the bear could breathe. Oh, but I knew this stuffed bear couldn't actually breathe, and that it wasn't really alive or a replacement for Isabelle. It was a symbol—as the woman from our support group had suggested—a visual reminder that there was another member to our family. It was human nature to forget about that which cannot be seen, and I couldn't let Isabelle become out of sight, out of mind.

* * *

Chad and I stayed home on New Year's Eve. Being pregnant, I definitely wasn't interested in the bar scene, and neither of us wanted to be around people who were celebrating. Instead, we watched the festivities at Times Square on T.V. from the comfort of our basement couch. We were both silent when the ball dropped. We didn't even say Happy New Year to each other or move in close for the traditional kiss. I knew what was going through my mind and I could imagine similar thoughts in Chad's head. We tended to think alike. Part of me just wanted to get out of this year and start a new year. Yet part of me wanted to stay in this year, because it was the year we had Isabelle.

As we watched the party-goers celebrate on T.V., we talked about the grand plans people made to be better or different in the New Year—how they made promises (and we were guilty of it, too) to go to the gym, or to eat better, or to treat others with kindness.

"This was the best year and the worst year of my life," Chad said. "I got my promotion at work and we had Isabelle. But, you went through that awful postpartum depression and we lost Isabelle."

I thought about the other good and bad aspects of the past year for me. "We also got pregnant again on the first try," I said, but that was, admittedly, a hard one to tally. When we made the decision to get pregnant again, we'd talked about the fact that we most likely wouldn't have tried to have another baby so soon if Isabelle were alive. It didn't seem fair to her or to the new baby to even talk about it again. And as I lay on the couch and tried to look forward to the New Year, the plans we'd make and the expected addition to our family, I felt afraid of what the next year might bring. Would I someday refer to this past year *and* the new one as the worst *years* of my life?

* * *

Chad and I were warned in our support group about people in our lives who would expect us to be "over" our loss when they thought enough time had passed. I mentally ran through our family members and friends to determine if I thought any of them would even hint at us "getting over" losing Isabelle. I couldn't think of one person, and maybe it was because I'd shared openly with just about everyone I knew that we didn't think there was anything to "get over." Early on, I came to terms with the idea that the grief of losing Isabelle would be like a backpack I'd carry with me for the rest of my life. Some days it would be like a heavy weight that would slow me down, and other days it would be like a light breeze that would push me forward.

But, our support group was right. There was one acquaintance who caught me off guard on the one day of the week I went into the newspaper office to compile police reports and calendars. Because I'd known some of the people at the paper for nearly a decade and enjoyed great relationships with others, they were extremely supportive when they heard the news about Isabelle. Most of them came to the funeral and checked in often to see how I was doing.

Innocently enough, one of the sales guys asked me how my New Year's Eve went.

I shrugged my shoulders without looking up from the computer and said, "It was fine. Kind of hard for us actually."

"Well, what'd you guys do?" he pressed on.

"Chad and I didn't do anything. We just hung out at home and watched a movie."

"Well aren't you a Grinch!" he yelped, shocking me enough that I looked up at him.

"We didn't feel much like celebrating," I said acidly. "I'm pregnant and—" with emphasis "—it's been a hard year for us."

"Well, get in the spirit, why don't ya?" he said and laughed, then he walked away laughing.

I analyzed the situation for a minute, but then let it go until later that night when I mentioned it to Chad. Having been prepared by our support group, and not really valuing the sales guy's opinion, we decided not to take it personally. Maybe he thought five months was the statute of limitation on grieving.

"It sounds like you gave him enough hints," Chad said. "He should've gotten it."

I shook my head. "Some people spin on their own axis, I guess, oblivious to what's happening here on earth."

Chad shook his head playfully. "Well aren't you just the pregnant Grinch now?"

* * *

When I scheduled the ultrasound for Baby Lyon on Chad's birthday, January 16, I did so because I wanted to try to help him somehow. I attributed his anger and sadness to the holidays, but as January crept on, his mood grew more and more dismal. Many Minnesotans succumbed to a condition known as Seasonal Affectiveness Disorder (SAD) because of the months and months without significant sunlight or warmth. I wondered if he was a candidate. I didn't begrudge his mood. We'd lost our child; there was no quick fix for that.

I felt like the lucky one, though, and felt guilty for feeling lucky. I had the Izzy Bell project to keep me busy and new life growing inside of me. This new relationship with God was developing that felt a bit like having a new friend. I slept in the spare bedroom most nights because our cushy pillow-top mattress hurt my back, and each night before drifting off to sleep I talked to God about my day and posed questions for him. I invited him to lead me with words such as, "Guide me, God. Where do you want me to take the Izzy Bell project?" and, "Show me the answers to the questions I have. Help me find the resources I need." And, for the most part, he did.

Chad and I were in the car on our way to the hospital for the ultrasound when he let out an exceptionally heavy sigh.

"There's a lot of thought in that," I said. I was driving, since I now got motion sickness as a passenger.

"Do you think we'll ever be happy again?" he asked, looking out the window.

"I'm happy!" I blurted a little too enthusiastically. Maybe I was trying to assure him, but most likely I was trying to reassure myself. Chad talked about how much he missed Isabelle, and said he was miserable and didn't think he would ever feel happy again.

"There are still a lot of things to be happy about," I said.

Chad shook his head. "I'm not even excited about the new baby."

I pressed my eyes closed for a split second. That just wasn't fair. He'd made that comment once before and I'd let it go. I let it go that day, too, because it was his birthday and we were finding out the sex of our baby and I didn't have the energy to try to make either of us feel better. Someone once told me that a woman becomes a mother when she finds out she's pregnant and a man becomes a father when he holds the baby for the first time. We were both parents already, but I felt a connection to this new baby. That would come for Chad over time, so I tried to accept that the day might not come for Chad until the day he or she was born. *God, let it be a she,* I thought.

"Isabelle sent this baby to us, Chad," I finally said, touching his arm. "I asked God and I asked Isabelle and that very month I was pregnant. They sent this baby to us."

Chad continued to look out the window.

We met Chad's mom at the hospital. My mom and sister were with us when we found out Isabelle's sex, and I thought it would mean a lot for Karen to be with us when we found out Baby Lyon's sex. It was no secret to anyone that Chad and I hoped desperately for a girl. We didn't want to change Isabelle's nursery and we didn't want to put away her clothes. Having a girl would be easier all around. I just hoped God understood how important it was to us.

The same ultrasound tech greeted us and, thankfully, she didn't seem to remember that we'd been there a year-and-a-half earlier. I waited, breath held, but she didn't ask about Isabelle. She also didn't ask if this was our first baby, as she had when we'd been in before. Maybe our chart now disclosed our loss with a big red sticker that said, "Warning! Bereaved parents!"

We were in the same room again, the jelly was cold again, and the pressure of the ultrasound device made me have to pee again. When I saw the figure moving on the screen, I smiled. A real, genuine smile that made my heart flutter. The baby was an acrobat and the ultrasound tech chased it around with the wand across my slippery belly as she struggled to document the presence of all body parts.

Karen didn't "ooh" and "ahh" as my mom and sister had, and Chad's face was expressionless as he looked at the screen. There was a bittersweetness in the air and no one seemed to know how to act, so I tried to be excited enough for all of us.

"Wow! Look at that little bugger go!" I chirped, and, "Holy smokes that's an active little one!"

The ultrasound tech broke my mood with the question I'd been dreading: "So, do you want to know the sex?"

I nodded and looked at Chad, who seemed to have an imaginary bubble over his head: *Girl, girl, girl.*

"Boy," she said flatly, and it really did feel like my bubble burst. Chad was silent and glanced over his shoulder at his mom.

The ultrasound tech said something about small traces of urine in the bladder that indicate a boy. I swallowed hard as she wiped the jelly off my belly.

"You can go wash up in the bathroom," she said.

I slipped off the table, hurried into the bathroom, swiped off my midsection, then hurried out. I took the printout of images she offered.

"Thank you," I said, and hustled out of the room with Chad and Karen behind me. I stared straight ahead, trying not to blink, trying not to think. Then I felt Chad touch my back and my resolve crumbled. I practically fell into him and the sobs literally choked me as I tried to hold them back. We walked out of the hospital with his arm around me. I heard him sniffle. He was crying, too. We didn't say anything in the car, but stopped at Walgreens so I could pick up more prenatal vitamins. I'd composed myself somewhat, but for some reason when I walked through the automatic doors, the tears rolled again. I rushed into the empty ladies room and let out a verbal assault on God.

"I told you I wanted a girl!" I hissed from the privacy of the handicap stall. "I needed a girl! Now I have to change her room and pack up her clothes and..." I hit the metal door with the palm of my hand. "What is wrong with you? Why can't you just do what I need you to do for once?"

I leaned against the cold tile wall and rubbed my belly. I felt a complete loss of control and considered sliding to the bathroom floor and curling up into a ball. It was a public restroom, though, and I'd seen a documentary involving black lights and rubber gloves, and that was enough to move me. I wiped my eyes, washed my hands twice, and stepped back into reality.

I wandered the aisles of Walgreens and eventually called Mom to tell her we were having a boy.

"Oh, Amy," she said, "That's so wonderful!" Mixed in with the excitement, I heard the hesitancy in her voice.

"Yeah," I said, "but her room, her things..." The tears fell again.

Mom remained upbeat. She reminded me that "God knows what he's doing even when we think we could do better if we were in charge." Maybe, she said, having a boy was part of the healing process for us, as the differences between a boy and a girl would be more evident. She thought maybe I wouldn't worry so much about comparing him to Isabelle.

"This really is great news, Amy," she said before we hung up. "Isabelle's going to have a brother!"

* * *

I was working on my taxes at the end of January, recording my expenses for my craft business, when I noticed a receipt from June 20 when Chad and I drove an hour-and-a-half west with Isabelle to buy a couple of kilns that were listed on Craigslist. The seller lived on a farm, and we wandered around and talked with him and his family for over an hour. I carried Isabelle and she was so curious about all of the activity. The memory put me into tears and I longed to hold her again and to smell the sweet mixture of baby shampoo and horse manure.

A few minutes later I found a receipt from Continental Clay and my breath caught in my throat. Isabelle and I had taken a trip to the Minneapolis shop on June 25 to look for glass-slumping molds, and she was more than accommodating—wide awake while we looked through the store, then fast asleep for the ride home. I remember thinking that I was the luckiest mom in the world.

Then I found another receipt for the business class I took with Marti on July 19, four days before Isabelle went into the hospital. Now I wished more than anything that I hadn't gone to that class and hadn't had that second glass of wine. Instead, I wished I would have spent the whole night at home cuddling her.

* * *

Upon further reflection, I realize my niece, Alexys, is the main reason I decided to have children. Chad and I were named her godparents when she was born, and we were able to see her in the hospital when she was one day old. I was twenty-eight, newly married, and had never held a baby that small (other than my baby sister when I was six years old). Watching Lexy grow was life-changing for me.

There was one day during my real estate tenure that I had felt particularly awful about my job. Maybe a closing fell through or maybe a buyer went with a different agent. Whatever it was, Chad had tried everything to cheer me up that evening, but nothing worked until he asked if I wanted to walk over to his dad's house, a block away, to see Lexy. She was eighteen months old by that time and I held her and played with her and immediately understood the magic a child could bring to your life. Whatever it was that ailed me, I was cured of my bad day.

So it was no surprise that I expected similar magic when Lexy stayed overnight at our house at the end of January. Isabelle had only been gone six months, but we offered to have Lexy stay the night when Andre and her husband, Neal, knew they had to be to work early the next morning. Now five, Lexy told us repeatedly that she wanted to sleep in Isabelle's room, which was especially difficult for Chad to hear since he hadn't spent any time in the room since her death. I was downstairs while Chad got Lexy ready for bed. He later told me that she was so excited to go inside Isabelle's room, but when she grabbed for the door handle, Chad felt himself freeze; and when she flipped on the light, he felt like he was somewhere else—beside himself and outside of himself.

Lexy chattered away about the trinkets in Isabelle's room, the pictures we displayed, and said, "Wow, Isabelle's got a lot of stuff on her walls!"

That's when I came in and Chad went out. He was crying and tried to shield himself from Lexy's view. He didn't want her to feel like she'd done anything wrong by celebrating Isabelle.

I had less intense reactions when I entered Isabelle's room, because I'd slowly worked my way up to spending time in there. I'd gotten in the habit of visiting the space a couple of times a week, sometimes just to sit for awhile in the beige rocking chair I'd sat in while I fed Isabelle or rocked her to sleep. Sometimes I sat in that chair and I thought about her and I cried, but I let the tears freefall because I knew the pain had to come out. And sometimes I'd talk through what I felt with God, and more often than not I got angry at him and wondered, "Why me?"

As I tucked Lexy into bed that night on the futon in Isabelle's room, I noticed that the room still smelled like Isabelle: new wood from her crib, fresh baby wipes, baby powder, and the sweet scent of her baby lotion.

Neither Chad nor I talked about it, but we knew it was true. The room would have to be cleaned up and changed for Baby Lyon. All of the toys and swings and baby bottles that had been scattered lovingly throughout the house before Isabelle went to Heaven were now stored in that room. Eventually those things would be placed throughout the house again and we'd have to enter the room daily, live in it. There would be life in it again.

The idea made me queasy with apprehension. Our new little boy—Wyatt, we would call him—was Isabelle's brother, and I really did believe Isabelle and God picked him out especially for us. On good days, I could almost envision God holding Isabelle's tiny hand as she peered around like she was shopping for something special. In my vision, Isabelle would stop, point, and offer God her giant prom smile. "There!" she would shout (because in Heaven she could talk). "Right there! He's perfect. That's my baby brother!"

But it would take us some time to understand.

Chapter Seventeen

Wyatt totally zapped my energy and caused me to have intense sugar cravings that drove me to Dairy Queen several times each week for cookie-dough Blizzards. On top of that, I was slammed in February with stories for the newspaper and I'd started freelance writing for Devicix for extra money. The engineers had caught wind of my writing background and paid me to write bios for their employees. I also created their company newsletter that would be sent out to their clients and taken to trade shows.

When I got home on a Friday afternoon in mid-February, I felt frazzled and anxious. I was doing too much. I rested on a blanket on the living room floor, closed my eyes, and focused on my breathing while listening to my "Ocean Surf" CD. I only sat in the position for about ten minutes because my mind wandered chaotically. I felt good when I got up, though, so I tried relaxing like that again the next day and the day after that. But when I tried relaxing on the fourth day, Raven started a war for attention with our two cats, which ended in Guinness, the fat black cat, seeking refuge on my lap.

Our bedroom was enormous with hardwood floors, and a corner of the room sat empty, collecting dust bunnies and dog hair. I dusted the floor, pulled out a purple oriental rug I'd stored in the closet, and moved an old boom box onto my nightstand. I shut the door to keep the animals out.

Mom had given me a tape set when I was sixteen called *Peaceful White Light*. The set contained six guided relaxations: "White Light Bubble," "Magic Garden," "Inner Guide," "Loved One," "Reminiscing," and "Ocean Waves." Mom was into alternative healing before the Western world capitalized on our quest for inner peace.

She thought the relaxing might help curb the anxiety that had crept into my life in high school. I thought it was a cool idea, but never got around to it.

But on that below-zero February day in my bedroom, I thought that some dedicated quiet time might help me to further connect with God, to "be still and know that he is God," as I heard Pastor Tom say once during a sermon. I got cozy on the floor and chose the session called "White Light Bubble." All of the tapes started the same way: with five minutes of guided relaxation aimed at loosening tensions from my head to my toes.

"Now, imagine you are in a special place. You are inside a large bubble!" the woman's soothing voice said, and my pulse kicked up a notch. I was claustrophobic and didn't like close spaces, real or imagined. But her voice continued to draw me in, and so in my make-believe world I created a little door through which I could exit from the bubble if need be. And just as I started to wonder what I was supposed to do inside the bubble, the little door flipped open and she was there. In my arms and in my bubble—*Isabelle!* Laughing. Smiling. Cooing. I knew I was smiling in real life. I was in my room, my eyes were closed, and I was smiling, but I was also in the bubble. Another part of me. In the bubble with Isabelle. We bounced and she floated, always within reach. I didn't talk to her. I just smiled and she smiled and we tumbled and laughed for an amount of time that was immeasurable. My happiness was immeasurable. When it was time for her to leave I was able to let her go, confident she would never be far away from me. Tears rolled down my cheeks. I was aware of the tears, even in my alternate state. And when I "awoke" at the tape's guiding, I was at peace.

That night I told Chad about my bubble experience and, after tearing up, he became visibly upset. "Why don't I ever see Isabelle? Or dream about her?" he asked.

I tried to comfort him by brushing off my experience as a product of my overly active imagination. He brushed me off, though, and said he was fine, then he went to the bar to watch the football game.

The next day I chose a relaxation tape called "Inner Guide," and opened myself up to what this quiet time might bring. I didn't try to control or manipulate it to be what I wanted it to be. Instead, the soothing voice guided me to meet the *person* who I believed guided my innermost thoughts. My guide's name was Amy and she looked a lot like me. She wore a white, gauzy, flowing frock and seemed to hover just above the ground, encircled by a glowing fog. I wasn't frightened by her, surprisingly, but I was intrigued. We sat on a bench in a garden surrounded by a white picket fence and I lay my head on her shoulder. My feet were bare and the grass felt nice on my skin.

"I'm glad we finally get to meet," she said. "I've always been with you, trying to steer you in the right direction."

I nodded.

"Sometimes you just don't listen," she said in a soft voice, "and sometimes I get frustrated."

I nodded but, again, was silent.

We sat awhile and she reassured me that I'd never be alone, even if there wasn't a single person around me. And in the distance I could hear a voice telling us that our time was winding down. Amy touched my hand as she stood to leave the garden. "I'm going to go now, but I'd never leave you," she said. "Just remember that."

* * *

I had no business start-up experience, but I was determined to press on with the Izzy Bell project. I wouldn't have known how to manage Lexy's ant farm let alone a brand new company, but that didn't stop me. It didn't help, though, that a former real estate colleague pointed out my inexperience with a resounding, "What makes you think you could start your own company?" about the same time my confidence was falling through the floor.

He was flabbergasted that I put my real estate license on ice and devoted my time to a mission called the Izzy Bell Advanced Baby Monitor.

"Who's helping you?" he probed with a furrowed brow.

I told him about Devicix and the development proposal they'd given me for a prototype just that week in hopes that he, too, would realize that I had brilliant engineers in my corner with more fancy degrees than a thermometer. I told him about my brother-in-law, who had a business and financial background, and about our lawyer with her sixteen-year track record of representing medical device companies and start-ups. I name-dropped and I tried to prove my worth to him, but my former colleague didn't seem impressed. I racked my brain for other names that I could throw out or impressive statistics from my business plan. As a last-ditch effort, I blurted, "Well, I've done a lot of research on the Internet—"

"What?!" His head flipped back and he howled. "You're going to learn how to run a company from the Internet? Is Sally Struthers teaching the class? Can you get your degree at home in your spare time?"

The stench of that conversation hung in the air for several days. I felt like a failure. I hadn't failed at anything, not even close, but I'd plunked myself into the bin with the 97 percent of start-up companies that failed each year. I needed help and I didn't know where to find it.

"You need a thick skin to run a business," Chad said that night, and his comment irked me more than anything. I felt alone in the project, and it made me feel even more alone that my husband holed up in the basement every night, cranky and depressed, and was seemingly uninterested in the whole project. I tried to share ideas with him, brainstorm, but I was met with blank stares and shoulder shrugs.

Mom came to the rescue the next day when she told me to take out a piece of paper and write down the things I'd accomplished and learned in the last six months.

"It's easier to look back and say, 'Wow, I have done a lot,' but looking forward into the unknown is very, very scary," I told her. "If I don't do this I have nothing." And in those words I realized that the Izzy Bell Advanced Baby Monitor resembled, for me, my last living link to Isabelle. The project sprang to life the day she went to Heaven and I felt I'd be a failure, a worthless mom, if I didn't keep it alive. And maybe this project could keep a part of me from dying as well.

I wasn't naïve enough to think that the road ahead of me wouldn't be bumpy, but luckily I was just oblivious enough to keep bouncing forward. It was with that revived mentality that I highlighted my inexperience in a request to the Minnesota-based Sophia Angel Fund, a group of thirty-some "angels" who invested in women-run companies in the initial stages of development. It was my first crack at approaching an investor and maybe it was good that I didn't know the statistics of how many companies these angels invested in per year or the status of other applicants who were likely a heck of a lot more qualified than me. And I didn't want to know. If someone like my former colleague could throw me off-kilter for two days, other discouraging comments would likely send me into another one of my I'm-not-worthy tailspins—and I needed to cut back on those. I was getting too old for tantrums.

Waiting really was the hardest part. Near the end of February, just after my thirty-second birthday, I got a call from Joy Lindsey, a prominent investor in the Sophia Angel Fund and a well-known name in the Twin Cities. Basically, the group shot me down. But the most surprising bit about the whole situation was that I didn't freak out. I picked Joy's brain for information about finding investors and asked how far along they needed me to be before I approached them again. She suggested my next step should be to obtain a working prototype.

I had a meeting with Chad that night and discussed how we might find the money to have a prototype created. It would be some sort of measuring device connected to a wearable blanket. We could put it on a doll or teddy bear and show that when a baby rolled over onto its stomach, the device could sound an alert to notify a caregiver to move the baby onto its back. We kicked around a few ideas but a solution was hard to find. Initial estimates from Devicix came in at $2,000 to $5,000. My freelance writing barely helped pay the bills and left nothing to spare. I needed to find that money, but I didn't know where.

I prayed out loud and talked to the baby in my belly the next night during the drive to hear some guy named Deepak Chopra speak. I'd heard the name before and I knew he was highly regarded by *spiritual experts,* so when I saw that he was speaking during a free event at a local church and signing his latest book, I felt compelled to attend.

The church was at capacity and my curiosity was piqued. Who was this Chopra character and why was the room buzzing with a vibrant energy? When he took a seat in the pew in front of me before the program began, and several camera bulbs flashed, I wasn't sure if I should be awe-struck by his apparent celebrity status, maybe reach out and touch the back of his shirt, or hide behind him so the pictures didn't show the pale, pregnant chic in the background.

When he got up to speak, I took note of his blue jeans, plain black shirt, red Nike tennis shoes, and sparkly red, Elton John-esque glasses. I was confused. I settled back in my seat and wondered if maybe with credentials like his he shouldn't have worn some sort of long robe or muted attire that conveyed prophet-like stature. For the next hour, Chopra spoke candidly and seemingly from his heart about spiritual healing, losing the fear of death, and living from our souls—which never die. And somewhere inside of that hour, he touched my soul.

As I walked across the parking lot holding my copy of his book, the phrase he'd closed with played in my mind: "What good is knowledge if you don't do something with it?"

I knew what I had to do. That night before going to bed, I composed a letter to Dad requesting money. It was hands down the hardest letter I'd ever written. Dad was sensitive about the subjects of giving, loaning, or spending money, and extremely smart when it came to investing and managing the family finances. Raised in an environment where no penny was wasted, I became extra mindful of money, too. I babysat and mowed lawns as an early teen, took a job as a dishwasher at a local restaurant when I was fifteen, and then stashed most of that money away in a savings account Dad had set up for me. And although my parents provided for all of my needs and nearly every one of my teenage wants, I struggled with asking for a handout. And Dad didn't give handouts. You worked for what you wanted, and if you didn't have the money, you found a way to get it or you didn't get what you wanted. Simple as that.

So, I posed my request to Dad as an investment. I gave him facts and figures, and even included a copy of the baby monitor business plan. I outlined what the money would be used for: the creation of a prototype, the legal fees of setting up our LLC, and maybe some initial fees for our provisional patent.

Three days later Dad called to tell me he'd cashed out one of his CDs and a check was in the mail. He didn't ask questions, didn't make me feel guilty about asking for the money, and I cried when we hung up the phone. I knew he believed in me. Who knew if he believed in the Izzy Bell project and its potential for success, but he believed that I believed and that was enough.

The next day I contacted Devicix and asked for an official prototype estimate. A few days after that I gave the engineers the go-ahead to start work, which they guessed would take about a month.

* * *

I spent most of March thinking about Isabelle's upcoming birthday on the twenty-seventh. Parents in our support group had shared ideas with us for activities they'd planned to celebrate a day that was traditionally cheerful, but hard to celebrate without the guest of honor. Ultimately, we called it "Isabelle's Celebration of Life," and invited

Chad's family over for a balloon release and cake. I took dozens of pictures that I sent to my family in Florida.

Our family went in together and surprised us with a star purchased in Isabelle's memory—located in her sign of Aries. Chad's dad gave us a wooden birdhouse in the shape of an angel to hang in Isabelle's Garden. Andre brought over sixteen pink balloons, and we used black markers to write messages on the balloons. It was interesting how each person found his or her own spot in the house or in the yard to think privately for a moment, then to write on a balloon. Andre wrote, "Izzy, I hope you're having fun in Heaven. I love you and can't wait to see you again." Chad's dad wrote, "Save a spot for me. Grandpa Lyon." Chad wrote, "I miss you Isabelle. You will always be a part of my heart. I love you. Daddy." Jennie wrote, "Remember to watch over your new brother." I wrote, "Have fun and play lots in Heaven. Mommy will see you soon and we can play together again. I love you baby girl. Mommy."

Out in the yard, huddled together for pictures with sixteen pink balloons, I felt like I was in the middle of a glorious ball of cotton candy. On the count of three, we released our balloons into the cloudless sky. They left our hands clustered together, and some rose quickly while others took their time.

"Look at them go!" someone yelled.

"There they are! Can you see them?" someone else shouted after the balloons had cleared the treetops without any popping. We cheered them on as if it was a race. First one to Heaven wins!

Chapter Eighteen

Chad and I picked up the prototype the first week in April. It was a fairly simple device to the tune of $2,700. Mom followed one of my drawings and expertly sewed a "wearable blanket" out of soft, yellow material. There was a small, Velcro front pocket that would hold the wireless monitoring device. The blanket zipped across the bottom and was sleeveless—similar to Halo Innovations' popular SleepSack, which zipped up the front. The wearable blankets replaced traditional blankets in the crib, an American Academy of Pediatrics' recommendation, because the garments were worn over pajamas or, in the summer, instead of pajamas.

I anxiously slipped the wearable blanket onto one of Lexy's Bitty Baby dolls, placed the tiny monitoring device into the pocket, and when we rolled the doll onto its stomach, the nearby box made a gentle dinging sound after 15 seconds, just like it was programmed to do. When Chad rolled the doll onto its back, the dinging stopped. There were no wires or cords. The monitoring was done remotely and the box that made the sound could be set next to a traditional baby monitor or used by itself. It was easily portable and would travel in a little pouch. I envisioned designer pouches someday for the "Yoga Mommies" and their "Hipster Babies." Additional wearable blankets with the special pockets would also be available. I had big plans and they got bigger with every ding of the monitor.

At home I placed the prototype in a special canvas box. But a momentary doubt needled me and I rubbed my belly.

Would I really use this on baby Wyatt? Did I really want to? And would it really work to prevent SIDS if doctors were still unsure what caused it?

More importantly, was I just using this to make losing Isabelle have purpose?

I shook my head. *How could I even think that? The monitor wasn't to prevent SIDS,* I reminded myself, *it was to help parents prevent some of the risk factors involved. And it did that.*

I closed the box and put the questions away.

For two weeks I brought the prototype and the doll everywhere we went, and I demonstrated the monitor for our family and friends. We were making headway and I was proud. Jen's friend Joa created, at no charge, an unbelievably adorable logo for Izzy Bell using a font that resonated playfulness and safety. The letters were two-toned green and the "I" was dotted with a heart. A sweet-looking bell hung overhead, seemingly dinging its encouragement. Using that logo, she designed letterhead, business cards, and even a banner that we could hang at trade shows. She said she was glad she could help. Then Jen surprised us with a box of business cards and said it was the least she could do to help. The support pushed me forward as I continued down a path that was completely foreign to me and at an altitude I had no business travelling through.

* * *

The Minnesota CUP Breakthrough Ideas competition was created for aspiring entrepreneurs and start-up companies to gain recognition and hopefully seed capital to move their businesses forward. It was a serious contest for serious people who knew what they were doing. I'd heard about the contest from my brother-in-law, Adam, who had entered a few years before with his super high-tech business software to curb identity theft. He was one of those math/statistics whizzes, and his company, ID Insight, placed second in the competition out of 600 entries. I was beside myself with awe when he told me the story.

"We lost to a company that created these recycled paver stones," Adam said. "It was actually pretty cool. They set up a sample walkway during the final round as part of their presentation. How could I compete with that? All I had to show was a software program."

He didn't seem bitter that he'd missed out on the contest's $20,000 in seed capital for the winner. His company was up and running and had recently landed Target stores as an account for credit card application verification. So when Adam insisted that I enter the Minnesota CUP competition, I listened to him. There were three rounds of judging, he explained. Round one required entrants to create high-level summaries of their ideas. If they passed on to Round Two (top thirty), they elaborated on their plans with a detailed proposal describing the aspects that made their ideas viable ones. Round Three consisted of the top five entrants, who would be called upon to give ten-minute presentations to the review board, which consisted of twenty esteemed business leaders from throughout the Twin Cities area.

"Wow," I murmured, feeling the insignificance of my experience like a heavy weight on my shoulders. Adam told me not to think that far ahead and encouraged me to focus on Round One.

"If nothing else, you'll come into contact with people who might be able to help you," he said.

I found more information about the contest on the Internet. In an online application process, I needed to develop an executive summary, a description of the product, a description of the market size and audience, and an operating plan. My leg bounced with excitement and nervousness under the table as I read the rules. I already had those sections ready to go. And then I read the words, "400-word maximum for each section," and my excitement tanked.

I held a hard copy of my business plan in front of me. The titillating read weighed in at approximately 9,568 words, not including graphs and tables. I didn't know how I could possibly pare the important factoids down to 1,600 words total, but I spent the last part of April and first part of May clipping and consolidating until I'd reached my version of perfection. I filled out the online application and on May 17, two weeks before Wyatt was expected, I clicked "Submit." My entry swirled away, where I imagined it would land among 600 or more other applications. I tried to put the Minnesota CUP Breakthrough Ideas Competition out of my thoughts, so it was a good thing then that I didn't know the number of entries had already skyrocketed to more than 850.

* * *

Saturday, May 31

Baby Wyatt is due to be born tomorrow. He's not showing any signs of moving from his comfy home with one foot lodged in my rib cage. His head is down, but he's been in that position for a few months. I tried bouncing around the yard for an hour today on the riding lawn mower (Chad appreciated that I cut the grass but worried the neighbors might think he was a slave driver) and tomorrow I'm going with Chad's mom and sister to stroll the Edina Art Fair. It's getting hot outside and I don't have any summer maternity clothes. I've been wearing Chad's clothes. The ensemble on the docket for tomorrow is a blue hippie skirt (mine, not Chad's) and my sweet husband's brown tank top of trailer-park style.

My sister-in-law, Andre, thought I should write a book about losing Isabelle, or some kind of guide for people who've struggled with how to comfort someone who has lost a loved one.

"I'm not an expert on grieving," I told her over dinner, two days past my due date. "I have no clue what's right or wrong."

"But look at all of these stories you've told me and all of the inappropriate things people have said to you," she said. "That would help people so much because no one knows what to say at a funeral. Or what to write in a card."

I sloughed off the idea for a while, but it stuck with me. I wrote and eventually submitted an article to a few magazines called "A Baby Lost: What Not to Say (or do) When You Don't Know What to Say (or do)." Writing the article made me think back to the visitor at the funeral who'd said, "You'll get over this someday," or Pixie the tattoo girl who'd compared losing Isabelle to losing her dog. I'd been so angry at her that morning in the tattoo shop, and had shared the story of her unfair comparison a number of times over the last year—baffled that she would ever think to relate her dog to my daughter. But recently I remembered the heartache I felt when my childhood cocker spaniel, Sam, died while we were away on a family vacation. He'd been sick, but that hadn't made his death any easier. Sam was a member of our family, another person as far as we were concerned. We set a place for him at the table for birthday parties and even outfitted him with a party hat. After his death, there was no consoling me for months—a freshman in high school who'd just lost one of the most important "people" in her world. My heart softened a little toward Pixie now. Her dog very well could have represented stability in what seemed to be an incredibly unstable world for her, and maybe he was the most important "person" in her life.

As my pregnancy had progressed, I learned not to be angry with inquisitive people who asked questions. At the grocery store, gas station, and even the movie theater: "When are you due?" "Do you know what you're having?" and, without fail, "Is this your first?"

I enjoyed the questions when I was pregnant with Isabelle, but that changed with Wyatt. In the end I had to tell the truth and that made most people uncomfortable. Society is encouraged by pregnant women. They carry inside of them the promises of new life, and the innocence and purity that accompanies wiggly, giggly, cooing babies. What no one expects to hear is that tragedy can so easily attach itself to such a holistic image. And so I tried to deliver my story with a semblance of grace. The world was practically starving for a taste of good news and a protruding belly usually promised a sweet slice of Heaven. I guessed that a good portion of the strangers who'd asked, and I'd shared with, later wished they'd minded their own business. Or maybe they'd wished the pregnant chick had had the decency to lie to them.

"Oh! And remember the old ladies at that party?" Andre reminded me as I went up for a second helping of mashed potatoes. I knew I would regret it. My body couldn't hold much food with my stomach squashed up into a third of itself. I'd be painfully uncomfortable in an hour, but I dove in anyway. Maybe the dollops would be just enough to squeeze the little bugger out.

"Oh yes, the ladies," I said as I eased down onto the chair. There wasn't much else to do with a baby heel lodged in my right ribcage and the constant urge to pee, so we reminisced a little about the cream of the crop of crappy comments. There was an "Outdoor Olympics" get-together at a friend's house just before my thirty-second birthday in February, and the day started with someone's nosy mother assuring me I would be fine sledding down an icy hill.

"I'm six months pregnant!" I spat, opening my jacket and showing off my bump. "Suppose I'd hit a patch of ice and land on my belly."

"I know you're pregnant," she said, pointing. "I can tell. You're huge. Even under that jacket. But you can still do things when you're pregnant, you know." She waved her hands, exasperated. "What is it with women these days? You think you can't eat this or you can't do that. When I was pregnant, I smoked a pack of Virginia Slims a day and drank whiskey sours!"

It was later that day at that same splendid event that a very old woman, older than the first old woman, beamed with joy when I took off my coat and she caught sight of the roundness under my shirt.

"Oh! Is this your first?" she asked.

"No," I said and sat down on the couch. I flipped through an issue of *Glamour* magazine, feeling anything but glamorous.

"Whacha havin'?" she asked, dipping a carrot into the ranch dressing on her plate and simultaneously shuffling across the room toward me.

I didn't make eye contact. "A boy," I said.

She rubbed her hands together. "What's your other one? How old?"

"A girl," I said, still looking down.

"How old?" she pressed.

I leaned back and met her eyes. Here we go. I didn't want to make this poor, old lady cry, but she couldn't take a hint. "My daughter, Isabelle, was four months old in July when she passed away."

The old lady clapped her disjointed hands together and said, "Oh, yes, on to the next one," then she shuffled out of the room.

I sat in silence trying to think of something that rhymed with "passed away"…, "cast away," "spazzed today," "ran to play." Did this lady think Isabelle ran to play? No, I clearly said she was four months old. Obviously she couldn't run to play.

Other experiences I had weren't as awful as the two old biddies at the party, but rather showed me a kinder, shockingly wonderful side of humanity. The first time I'd met Ruby was a little over a year before. She was one of my melted glass customers. I was pregnant with Isabelle the first time I met Ruby, and when she arrived at the house with her little one, there I was five months pregnant again. Being ever friendly, she asked about "my baby" as she showed off her smiley two-month-old boy. I pointed to the baptism picture above the television and told her Isabelle's story. I only got one sentence out before Ruby started to cry—sob, actually. I apologized and begged her to stop. I didn't want her to upset her baby.

"Oh God, I'm so sorry," Ruby said as she wiped her eyes, mascara everywhere. "I can't even imagine." And then she cried more, probably because she did imagine. I wondered if maybe she had a little case of postpartum depression, but then I saw her look down at her little boy and realized she was imagining what it would be like to lose him.

"Well, I'm pregnant again!" I said, rubbing my belly. God only knows why I always felt I had to change the subject. "I'm having a boy this time."

Ruby perked up slightly, and after she left, I chastised myself for what I'd done; I'd minimized my loss to try to spare her feelings. And I did it all the time. I apologized repeatedly for sharing the sad news about Isabelle, and sometimes rambled on about the support we received from family and friends. Once I told a lady I went to support group meetings, just so she'd stop hugging me.

I quickly became exhausted around my seventh month from the weight of Wyatt and from telling my story, Isabelle's story. I became more of a homebody and ventured out as little as possible. I even scheduled my eye exam and haircut for the same day, hoping my stars would align in such a way that no one would ask me about my past, my present, my future, or my belly. But my stars were out of whack. I was hit with a double whammy that day.

The technician who tested my eyes for new contacts was very friendly and helpful. She informed me that women's eyes sometimes changed for the worse during pregnancy, then reverted to normal after childbirth.

"Interesting," I said. "Another wrinkle for my brain."

"Is this your first?" she asked, pointing to my belly.

I shook my head.

"Your second, huh? Do you have a boy or a girl at home?"

That was a new twist. No one had added "at home" before. She was sly. I gave her the details she requested and she stared blankly at me for a moment, then her face turned into a grimace. She completed the puff test in my eyes and the field of vision exam, then sat down across from me.

"I actually had a child pass away, too," she said and my heart sank. She didn't look up. Just wrote notes on my chart. "I was twenty, and four-and-a-half weeks along. I got this bad pain in my stomach and just thought I was having a really bad period. I didn't even know I was pregnant. I didn't plan it or anything. It dropped in the toilet like this big blood clot. I didn't know what it was till my doctor told me that I was probably pregnant."

I took a deep breath and said, "I'm sorry for your loss."

She nodded and lowered her head. "Yeah, it was really hard."

So, it wouldn't be hard to imagine why I dreaded my upcoming hair appointment later that afternoon at a new salon. I anticipated the line of questioning that would begin the moment I plopped down in the chair, my seven-month belly proudly protruding under the cape.

Was it a prerequisite of hairdressers to make idle chit-chat, and was it rude for a person to sit down, hold up her hand, and say, "I'm not in the mood for talking today"?

As expected, Heidi, a trendy little thing with smoky black hair, commented on my shirt and remarked how hard it was to find cute maternity tops like the one I wore. Then the questioning began and I answered in short snippets, sure we'd skated over the issue until she asked, "So, how old is your daughter now?"

"Well, actually, my daughter passed away in July," I said, then caught my awkward grin in the mirror, clearly trying to soften the blow.

Heidi's face went blank and she only paused slightly while cutting my hair. She caught my eyes in the mirror, shook her head, and snorted. "F---!" she spat and exhaled sharply. "Life just isn't f---ing fair, is it?"

The next hour of conversation was the most genuine to date. Heidi had never lost a baby, but she did have a daughter. She didn't try to minimize, maximize, process, or come to terms with my pain. She didn't spend several minutes formulating the perfect response. She just said what she felt at that exact moment—and that was a time-halting, room-silencing "F---!" Sometimes, there's not much else you can say.

* * *

Wyatt arrived Wednesday, June 4, at 3:27 a.m.

3:27 a.m. 3–27. Isabelle's birthday.

When the doctor wrapped him in a towel and set him on my chest I couldn't believe the love I felt.

"He's so little!" I cried, happy tears racing down my cheeks toward his little body.

"Oh, he's not little," the doctor laughed. "I'd guess eight or nine pounds."

A nurse suctioned Wyatt's mouth and watched intently as he parted his lips like a little fish out of water. No cry erupted like I'd expected, and just as the worry crept up my spine, the nurse quickly scooped him from my arms.

"He's having trouble transitioning," she said to the other two nurses and I looked to my doctor who didn't move, just stared at the flurry of blue scrubs at the other side of the room. He wasn't smiling anymore, and I watched his face just as I watched the faces of flight attendants during turbulence. If they didn't panic, I didn't panic. The doctor's expression was blank. I looked to the nurses, hands moving quickly. Blank. Someone made a phone call and a tall, male nurse in his mid-thirties arrived. He popped the ear pieces of his stethoscope into his ears, placed the round disk on Wyatt's chest, and squinted his eyes. Then he poked and prodded my son, almost shaking him.

I lay in the bed, unable to move my lower body as four nurses hovered over the warming table. My mind screamed, *He's going to die. I knew this would happen. He's going to die. Just like Isabelle.* I saw the male nurse pat Wyatt assertively on the butt as another nurse suctioned his throat. I waited for a cry, but there were no noises coming from my little guy. Chad stood between the bed and the nurses. I wondered if he was trying to block my view and that irritated me.

"Is he okay?" I asked, my voice cracking. I tried to push him aside.

"I don't know," Chad said, fear as thick as tar in his voice.

"He's having trouble transitioning," the nurse said to another tall man who rushed into the room.

"What does that mean?" I hissed, but no one heard me.

Finally one of the nurses announced that they were taking Wyatt to the Level Two Center and Chad should go with them.

"I'd rather be safe than sorry," a nurse said and I stared at her, unable to find my words. It seemed the epidural had numbed my tongue as well. My mind, however, raced to the worst possible scenario. *The Level Two Center? Are you taking him there to die so I won't see him and go crazy and try to get out of the bed?*

Suddenly they were gone. The room that had been cluttered with nurses, doctors, and the promise of new life was empty except for me. I couldn't move. I couldn't get up. All I could do was wait. I panicked when I thought about the moments preceding this unwanted alone time. The doctor had taken a while to get to the room. Wyatt was forced to stay put in the birth canal and I was told not to push, "not even a little bit." The position didn't sit well with Wyatt, and his usual heartbeat of 140 to 150 at routine doctor's visits dropped into the 50s. A nurse rubbed the top of his "crowning" head to "stimulate" him while we waited for the doctor.

I heard the heart monitor and I heard how slow the beats were. I was going to push. I was going to push just to get him out of there, and I would reach down and I would grab him myself and he would be okay because he would be with his mom. Moms always made everything okay. My heart rate skyrocketed as Wyatt's beats slowed. The nurse put an oxygen mask on me and told me to take deep breaths. I did as I was told and watched the door for the doctor, who eventually arrived with sleep marks on his face.

Alone in the room now, I glanced at the clock. It had been fifteen minutes since they'd taken Wyatt to the Level Two Center. My body began to shake uncontrollably. The nurse had told me earlier that I might get the shakes due to the drop in hormones and the rush of adrenaline. I knew the drill. I shook like I was electrified during the last half of my labor with Isabelle. The shaking caused the entire bed to move now, and as I started to cry it became nearly impossible for me to breathe. I was alone and I was scared to death...of death.

"God and Isabelle," I said out loud, clenching my trembling hands together, imagining my little girl sitting on the Lord's lap. "I can't lose him. Please don't let me lose him."

The tears tumbled from my eyes as I realized I didn't even want to say his name for fear of attachment. It was too late, though. I was already in love with Wyatt.

"I can't lose him, God," I whispered. "You and Isabelle sent him to me. Please don't let me lose him."

Chapter Nineteen

After my desperate prayer, I released my sweaty grip on the metal railings, sank back into the pillow, and managed to suck in a deep breath. Within seconds, my shakes disappeared. I scanned the room, confused. There was a surreal quality about the place that was both frightening and comforting. *Am I really here?* I wondered. *Did I shake to death? Am I dead?* Just then, the nurse I liked best swept into the room. A blur in blue.

"Wyatt's going to be just fine," she said and rushed to my side to rub my arm. "They have a pulse oximeter on his little pointer finger and his oxygen level is at 100 percent. He's breathing fine on his own and they're going to bring him back down to you in a few minutes. He's already exhibiting a little rooting reflex. I think he's hungry!"

I stared at her for a moment and my eyes filled with tears. "It's just so scary, you know—"

She nodded and continued to rub my arm. "I know."

* * *

We stayed an extra day in the hospital. I'd called our insurance company for clearance and they'd agreed to cover us fully because of our middle-of-the-night arrival. Most people rushed to get out of the hospital setting, but I liked my room at St. Francis. I had a private bathroom, large television, and plush chair easily converted to a sleeping bed for Chad. Truthfully, I also liked having breakfast, lunch, and dinner delivered to my bedside and taken away when I was finished. St. Francis didn't serve the traditionally bland hospital fare, but rather offered a full menu ranging from breakfast omelets, salads, and soups to sandwiches, pastas, and entrees. They even brought me hot chocolate with whipped cream.

I was also a little afraid to go home. Under the halo of St. Francis, I had nurses on hand who would insist I rest and relax rather than work or do chores. They stood at attention for signs of postpartum depression, and, most importantly, they could be there in a moment's notice if Wyatt stopped breathing. The last day in the hospital, I asked Chad to busy himself elsewhere for the afternoon so I could sleep and enjoy time alone with Wyatt. The poor thing had been circumcised that morning, was given baby Tylenol, and was expected to sleep most of the day. So we dozed, interrupted way too frequently by nurses, custodians, and some guy who wandered into the wrong room.

Each of the nurses who'd attended to us over the three days commented on the picture I had on the bedside table of Isabelle looking up at me while I held her close to my chest. She was only a few weeks old when the photo was taken. I appreciated that I didn't have to tell them my story. They already knew about Isabelle's journey to Heaven. My favorite nurse informed me that, as each shift ended, they shared our "history" with the incoming nurse if she wasn't already aware that we'd lost a baby. I liked that they openly talked about Isabelle with me and when I made comments about the differences in my pregnancies and deliveries, they didn't even flinch.

I found it interesting, and a little discouraging, that none of the nurses, doctors, or even our new pediatrician discussed the use of an apnea monitor or broached the subject of SIDS. Luckily I'd done enough research on my own to know that SIDS wasn't thought to be hereditary. In fact, I'd read that the death of a second baby seemingly due to SIDS often prompted an investigation into the parents for potential homicide. The statistic gave me little comfort, though, despite the rarity of a second loss. I'd lost Isabelle, so I felt my chances hovered right around 100 percent.

Chad and I had already discussed apnea monitors and tests that purportedly focused on risk factors associated with SIDS. I'd read in more than one report that those tests were inconclusive. We didn't want either. As far as we were concerned, an apnea monitor would drive us crazy because a newborn's breathing tended to be erratic anyway. Plus, inconclusive tests to determine risk factors for a cause of death that is still such a mystery would only double our anxiety. Suppose one of those tests showed a high risk in one area or another. I would never leave Wyatt's crib side. Instead, I asked, actually begged, God and Isabelle to keep a close watch over Wyatt. I put my faith 100 percent in God, and even though it was scary to give up the control (which I clearly never had in the first place) I knew I'd made the best decision for my family and me.

* * *

I was pretty impressed with myself when we got home. I found it very easy to lounge around, and to give Wyatt the attention he deserved and to give myself the rest I required. Chad called the living room "Ground Zero," because the area was littered with baby blankets, snacks, and all of the necessities required for constant mother-baby comfort.

The first night home I made up the futon in the nursery with the bassinet close by—just as we'd done with Isabelle. But when I lay down, exhausted and ready to sleep, my mind reeled with memories. I looked around the room, lit by the same dim turtle light, and I heard the same tick-tock from the clock. My breathing quickened, becoming shallow, and a quilt of mixed emotions covered me. I felt overwhelmed by my longing for Isabelle, and overcome by my love for Wyatt. I also felt guilt-ridden for the time I'd lost with Isabelle to postpartum depression and ashamed that I'd bonded so quickly with Wyatt. I worried that Isabelle had gotten the short end of the stick thanks to me and my issues. Sure, I'd been an acceptable mom, but I was absolutely clueless about how to care for a newborn. Was it fair to her that I'd had a steep learning curve and, because of my experience with her, I wasn't afraid to pick up Wyatt or change his diaper? I wasn't afraid he would break if I held him wrong, and I wasn't afraid that I couldn't love him. I was scared to death, however, that I might lose him the same way I'd lost her, and that's what pushed me over the edge that night. I lay on the futon for twenty minutes sobbing, then went downstairs to talk to Chad.

As I descended the stairs, Chad turned quickly. "What's wrong?" he asked, practically leaping from the recliner.

"No, no," I said, waving my hand, knowing he thought the worst.

As always, Chad was supportive and tried to fix the situation. We moved the bassinet into our bedroom, but our king-size bed was so high off the ground that it was a pain for me to get out of bed every time Wyatt fussed. With the futon, I could simply roll over and scoop him into my arms. Over the next couple of weeks, convenience and exhaustion won out, and I came to terms with sleeping in the nursery. I reminded myself nightly that my little angel was in Heaven, probably beaming her glorious prom smile at how quickly I'd fallen in love with her brother, the baby she'd picked out for us.

Chad and I spent a lot of time in the first two weeks watching Wyatt during his naps, not so much to make sure he was breathing, but to watch his facial expressions. When he smirked or smiled in his sleep, Chad and I were sure Isabelle was telling him a story or singing to him. Sometimes we joked that she was flying around with her little angel wings, bumping into things because she had her mother's coordination.

* * *

June 16 snuck up on us and the red star on the calendar reminded me that the Minnesota CUP Breakthrough Ideas announcement would come that day. I refreshed my e-mail inbox every five minutes for news from the competition's organizers, and when an e-mail did appear just after two in the afternoon, I jumped up from my seat.

"I can't open it!" I yelled to Chad in the living room, startling Wyatt. He didn't cry, thankfully. "I don't want to know. I don't want to know!"

Chad placed Wyatt on the floor and rushed into the dining room where I stood next to my laptop, waggling my finger at the screen.

Chad looked at the subject line. "Well, it says, 'Congratulations Minnesota CUP Semifinalists,'" he said, and grabbed for the mouse.

I pulled the mouse away from him. "But they're not congratulating *me* specifically," I said. "They're just saying congratulations to the semifinalists. You are not one of them, Amy, but here's a list of the semifinalists just so you know."

Chad gently pushed me aside, clicked open the e-mail and read out loud: "Dear Minnesota Cup Entrant. It is our honor to inform you that you are a semifinalist in the Minnesota—"

"I am! I am!" I screamed and tears filled my eyes. Chad and I hugged and when I looked at him he was teary, too.

He went on to read the entire e-mail as I paced the living room chanting, "I can't believe it! I can't believe it!"

"Wow, there were 854 entrants," Chad said. "And only thirty were chosen to be semifinalists."

"I feel like I won the lottery!" I yelled and scooped up Wyatt, inhaling his delicious baby scent. "We did it, buddy!"

Chad forwarded the e-mail to his family members and I called Mom at work. That evening as I sat on the bench in Isabelle's Garden with Wyatt tucked into a thin, quilted blanket, I told him how much being a semifinalist meant to me.

"This totally validates the Izzy Bell project for me," I said, rocking back and forth with him. "Even if I don't win the whole thing… Well, hopefully I'll win the whole thing, but if I don't…I know I made the right decisions." He cooed at me and I stroked his cheek. "You were definitely a right decision. You're good for my heart, buddy."

I admired the flowers in Isabelle's Garden, felt the wind gently brush the hair from my forehead, and believed I knew what it meant to follow God's plan for me. Would I have felt that way if I hadn't been a semifinalist? Maybe not. But I did feel that way that day and refused to discount my feelings. More importantly, I felt the bond between God and me growing stronger. Sometimes I loosened, sometimes he tightened, but overall we grew closer. Somewhere over the last year it had become commonplace for me to look to God for guidance on a daily basis, or to ask for his presence during something as simple as a trip to the store with Wyatt when I felt uneasy. I even thought that some of the innocent Christians I'd deemed "Jesus Freaks" maybe weren't such freaks after all. Maybe I was the one who'd had it wrong all along.

* * *

There was a semifinalist reception a week later, at which time I was given more information about the next round of the competition. A follow-up e-mail from the coordinators explained that Round Two would involve a thoroughly researched business plan, which I already had, but would have to whittle down to twenty pages. After that, five finalists would be chosen to move on to Round Three, an oral presentation to the judges. Finally, the winner would be chosen in early September. Obviously winning the whole shootin' match was my goal, but I was so excited to make the first cut that I urged myself to relish a little longer my good fortune.

Mom came from Florida for two weeks to meet and play with her new grandson. During her stay, I spent a considerable amount of time cutting and tweaking the business plan to slash the thirty-seven pages down to the required twenty pages. Cutting each page was torturous for me. The words were gospel, and the sentences strung together were my music, bringing deeper meaning and clarity to my song: the Izzy Bell Advanced Baby Monitor. To cut even one note seemed to disrupt the whole tune. The organizers of the Minnesota CUP competition were explicit in their directions, though. Any business plan of more than twenty pages would be discarded and the entrant disqualified.

It was easy for me to get wrapped up in my work, which often happened when I was writing, and I had a tendency to completely lose track of time and place. I tried to be exceptionally cognizant of the amount of time I spent each day on the business plan. I strived for discipline and balance. I'd learned my lesson. And if the time ticked away to more than three hours, Mom either peeked into the room with Wyatt and sang, "Somebody wants to play with his mommy," or, if I'd had a rough night with him and had gotten very little sleep, she was a bit more demanding in her instruction that I stop working, take a nap, and she would feed him a bottle of my pre-pumped breast milk. Mom's presence was good for my soul. Her companionship put my life in order, and on those rare occasions when both Mom and Kim could visit together, my world felt complete. My sister cheered me on from afar, though, with daily check-ins on my business plan status.

One added bonus of being a semifinalist included connection with a mentor who would look over my condensed business plan and offer feedback. I was nervous and anxious to meet Lee Jones via email. I'd read her profile and knew she was a woman with more than twenty years of healthcare and medical device industry experience, and she had worked for Medtronic for fourteen years. She sat on a handful of boards and offered counsel to prominent groups. After digesting my business plan for two days, Lee Jones gave me valuable feedback, but most importantly she pointed out the gigantic elephant that had taken up residence next to my kitchen table. She wanted to know what I didn't know: How was I planning to get my product into a retail giant such as Target? Or Wal-Mart? Or Babies R Us? What was my plan? Who were my connections? Admittedly, I didn't have the answers, and I scoured the Internet for help. Chad merely shrugged his shoulders when I asked for his thoughts, and even with my creative prose, I couldn't spin a good enough tale to answer Lee's burning questions.

I remembered a story I'd written for a magazine that year about a Minnesota couple who grew a great business out of selling pinecones.

Brian, one of the owners, had a yard full of pinecones and used them as fire starters in the winter. He wondered if coating the cones with wax would create exceptional kindling, and thus became the FireCones sold at Target by his company, Lightstone. In following years, he went on to create AromaCones for decorative purposes and the business moved into a gargantuan warehouse that popped out millions of wax-covered pinecones each year.

I remembered the nice, easy conversation I'd had with Brian and his significant other, Sherri, after the interview I'd done for the magazine. I'd told them about Isabelle and my hopes to create my own company with our first product, an advanced baby monitor. They encouraged me and offered to answer any questions that might threaten to stop me along my journey. With the deadline for Round Two looming only a few days away, I took them up on their offer. I e-mailed Brian, told him about my business plan, the prototype, and the placement in the competition. He promptly e-mailed me back and, after a few rounds of phone tag, we connected.

My fifteen-minute chat with Brian was invaluable. He told me some of the mistakes he and Sherri had made when they first started out, and how he would do things differently if given the chance. He told me about manufacturing reps and how they received a percentage of the margin, usually 2-to-5 percent.

"A good manufacturing rep," he said, "makes the first contact with a buyer like Target, then essentially should hold your hand through the compliance, shipping, labeling, and contract issues that will inevitably come up."

Brian said that a manufacturing rep would help make projections for what the stores would sell. In fact, Brian was meeting with a gentleman the following Monday who used to be a buyer's rep for Target and his wife still worked with Target.

"I'll mention you and your product," he said. "Hopefully you can connect."

I hung up the phone, snuggled Wyatt, and thought about dot-to-dot puzzles. The dots had connected quite perfectly since I'd made the decision to quit real estate and pursue the baby monitor. Each time I feared I'd reached my last dot without coming full circle, another dot appeared.

"This is really what you want me to do, isn't it God?" I whispered, feeling almost lucky that he'd entrusted me with such a huge project.

What other reason could God possibly have had for bringing me this far on the baby monitor journey?

Chapter Twenty

Tuesday, July 22

This is the week Isabelle passed away one year ago. The hurt is so raw that it could have been yesterday that she went to Heaven. Even the atmosphere feels the same. Thick. Sticky. Deadly. I feel superstitious. I won't go near the library since I was at the library before Chad called with the news that she was being airlifted. I refuse to wear that black tank top I wore that day, but I won't throw it away either. I just want out of this week and on to the next, even though that just means we're getting closer to "SIDS Time" with Wyatt. Most cases occur between two-and-four months.

There's no hiding from the terror that it could happen to Wyatt. I know that statistics and chances say that it won't happen again, but I don't gamble anymore.

Faith is hard to find in moments like these, but probably most important in moments like these. I ask God and Isabelle to watch over Wyatt when he's awake and when he's asleep, and to give me patience and clarity when I seek answers to questions that may go unanswered... at least in this lifetime.

In mid-August I found myself in a familiar situation: in the dining room, gazing at my laptop, waiting for an e-mail from the Minnesota CUP organizers.

"I have a bad feeling about this," I whispered to Wyatt as I bounced him on my knee.

I knew my manufacturing and distribution section lacked the stability necessary to move my product forward. I hoped, though, the judges could skim over my creatively written prose and believe I actually had a clue about how to get my baby monitor into a big box retailer. I didn't receive an e-mail in the afternoon, and by mid-evening I knew what that meant. Chad and Wyatt went to bed, but I stayed up until nearly midnight, refreshing my inbox every fifteen minutes.

Finally, the e-mail came through:

"Dear Amy,

Thank you for participating in this year's Minnesota Cup and congratulations on becoming a semi-finalist. The level of competition this year was very good. We received a great many compelling plans. Those that moved on to the final round all included strong breakthrough ideas, excellent details on how the idea would get to market and they were well presented.

Unfortunately, your entry did not move on to the final round.

They didn't provide in-depth feedback, but they did share a few observations of the reviewers: The plan was well written and presented, and there was positive feedback about the brand. The product concept and implementation appeared to be strong and have a strong potential market. The plan did a "very nice job" in outlining the competitive environment. However, with retail distribution being so important, the operating details around how I'd get the product into retailers' channels "was very light."

I moped around the house for a good week-and-a-half, but by the beginning of September, I was back at the computer researching and studying ways to bring a new product to the market. My resiliency surprised me. But that didn't mean I didn't feel frustrated by the project. Sometimes I felt as if I was failing Isabelle, like if the project wasn't a success and I stopped trying, then maybe it would seem like I didn't really miss her.

I tried to make my predominantly right-brained mentality understand the less-than-creative rules and regulations surrounding patents, infringements, claims, and specifications, words I never would have lumped together a year ago. And although I could proudly admit that I had the unique ability to learn just enough of most things to get by, I also had to concede that what I needed to learn to move the Izzy Bell project forward was much bigger than me and any knowledge I could gain from online tutorials and library books. I had to be honest with myself. Was it the best use of my talents, skills, and abilities to agonize over how to bring a product to the market when the best I could hope for was surface knowledge and luck? I'd never have the deep understanding that took other people years, decades even, to acquire. I was at a crossroads and had the distinct feeling I would set myself up for failure if I continued by myself.

So I relaxed with quiet time and did some soul searching on the matter. I asked myself what I really wanted from the Izzy Bell project. I knew I wanted to make a difference. Not in a cheesy, beauty-pageant-queen-wants-to-save-the-world way, but from the deepest part of myself. I wanted to save babies' lives. I had the energy and the drive, but did that really make a difference? When it came down to it, I knew I couldn't marry my present passions of being a writer and good mother with being a start-up business owner, patent expert, manufacturing guru, marketing specialist, and everything else that needed to be combined to get the Izzy Bell project off the ground. There were people who had brought new products to commercialization before. I didn't have to reinvent the wheel, but I did need help.

"God, is this really what you want me to do?" I prayed one afternoon, doubting myself and what I believed was God's plan for me. "If this is it, please give me the tools."

I e-mailed Bill Schmid, the founder of Halo Innovations, whose building was, coincidentally, mere blocks from the newspaper office. I took that as a sign. When I'd applied for assistance from the Sophia Angel Fund, Joy Lindsey had mentioned Bill. She said she was an investor in his company that created the SleepSack and that we had similar stories.

"The two of you should definitely talk," she'd said. "Feel free to mention my name."

I wasn't ready at that time, but I was ready now. I learned from his Web site that Bill had lost his daughter, Haley, to SIDS in 1991, after which he began researching sleeping environments. He started Halo Innovations in 1994 with a crib mattress offering unique ventilation and filtration options. The mattress didn't take off so well, he later told us, but when he introduced the SleepSack, a wearable blanket that replaced the need for sheets and quilts in the crib, business boomed.

I sent a message to Bill and received an e-mail the next day. He expressed his sympathy for our loss, but applauded our efforts to join in the fight against SIDS. He said it was interesting "how the hands of fate sometimes steer us," as he'd been toying with a monitor idea for some time as well. Bill and I went back and forth over the confidentiality agreements, both of us trying to protect ourselves, but eventually came to an agreement. Chad and I, with baby Wyatt in tow, met with Bill two weeks later in the conference room of Halo Innovations.

"First, I want to tell you how amazing it is that you're doing all of this after such a great loss," Bill said, and we proceeded to share our stories, the details that only another SIDS parent could understand. Even after seventeen years, I saw the pain in Bill's eyes and he winced at the raw details of our story.

Later, as we discussed our thoughts and ideas for a baby monitor, Bill seemed just as excited as we were. And by the end of two-and-a-half hours, I offered him a copy of our business plan. He promised to review it in the coming week during plane flights to and from a conference where he would learn more about recent SIDS research.

Chad went to work after the meeting and I allowed myself to spend a good portion of the afternoon fantasizing about forming a partnership with Halo. Chad was concerned about potentially losing the Izzy Bell identity, but I wasn't, not anymore at least. By then, I was determined to do what needed to be done to get the baby monitor out there. The name was just a cosmetic detail. No matter what the name ended up being, it would always be the Izzy Bell to us.

* * *

Wyatt was extra handsome on his four-month birthday when we took him to an outdoor festival at his cousin Nick's school. He donned the sunglasses Isabelle got for her baby shower even though they were a bit girly: yellow with sunflowers decorating the frame. We offset the shades with an oh-so-boy Nike jogging suit and tennis shoes. He was my little Joe Cool. I spread a blanket on the grass, and Wyatt and I played on our tummies, relishing what would probably be one of the last nice days of fall.

Andre rushed up to us. "Carla's here," she said.

"Where?" I asked, rising to my knees and scooping Wyatt into my arms. I adjusted my sunglasses. "Where is she?"

Andre pointed to a corn dog stand, and there, with children swarming all around her, Carla talked with another adult. Her kids went to the same private school as Andre's, so it shouldn't have surprised me to see her there. I could feel Andre watching me as I rose to my feet with Wyatt and walked in Carla's direction. Somewhere in the short distance Chad caught up with me.

Carla did a double take when she saw us. "Hi guys," she said.

I turned Wyatt around to face her. "I wanted you to meet Wyatt," I said.

Carla smiled and I held Wyatt out to her so she could hold him. Chad made some friendly comments about the memorial garden and Wyatt's developments. I grew antsy, though, unable to swallow the polite chit-chat. I knew we were all thinking about Isabelle, but no one was talking about her. She was what we all had in common.

"We're okay," I blurted in the middle of Chad's sentence, forgetting the polite nuances of adult conversation. "I mean, I miss Isabelle every single day and I know I will for the rest of my life, but…I mean, we're okay."

Carla nodded like my random ramblings made perfect sense to her. She told us she had wanted to close her day care, and maybe she would have if her daughter, Wendy, had been older.

"I was so overprotective of Caitlan," she said, and I remembered the infant who'd arrived at her day care when Isabelle was about three months old. "I didn't want to take care of any more babies."

I took Wyatt back from her and she told me that the county's day care licensing agency had listed SIDS information on its Web site as a result of Isabelle's death. I thought that was good. It was something. Maybe the information would not only raise awareness about safe-sleep practices and infant CPR, but also save lives.

We said our goodbyes and I returned to the spot in the grass. I fed Wyatt a bottle and rubbed the blonde fuzz on top of his head—so different from Izzy's dark hair. He curled into me and his eyes fluttered as he strained to stay awake. In the bright daylight I could see that his blue eyes—which had looked so much like mine when he was born—were turning brown like Chad's and Isabelle's. There would be so many changes in the coming months and years, and I said a silent prayer to God that he would keep my baby safe.

* * *

I read a news report the following week about the "simple" thing parents could do to reduce their infant's risk of SIDS. Researchers interviewed mothers of 185 infants who died from SIDS, and mothers of 312 infants of similar race and age. The mothers answered dozens of questions about their babies' sleeping environments. Researchers took into account other risk factors and found having a fan circulating air in the room where the baby slept was associated with a lower risk of SIDS. Moreover, very few of the babies who died from SIDS had a fan on in the room during their last sleep, the mothers reported. I wasn't convinced by the information, but I did appreciate that research continued to suggest that re-breathing air and not getting enough fresh oxygen could be fatal for babies who were prone to a SIDS death—whatever the causes were. More than ever, I thought that Bill at Halo was really onto something thirteen years before when he created the crib mattress that circulated fresh air.

That night, Chad installed a ceiling fan in Wyatt's room.

* * *

The temperature rapidly turned colder in mid-October. Although winter had always been a dreaded season for me, I couldn't help but feel velvety warm inside because the staff of Halo Innovations had reviewed my business plan and "found it favorable," according to an e-mail from Bill. They wanted to move forward. I worked diligently with our patent attorney, Suneel Aurora, to assemble a seventeen-page provisional patent titled, "MONITORING SYSTEM FOR DETECTING ROTATIONAL MOVEMENT OF THE BODY, DROPS OR FALLS, OR PHYSIOLOGICAL CONDITIONS." I was super-impressed with the finished product. I believed our provisional patent was fairly unique when compared to "prior art," as previous patents were called. Our provisional patent came complete with the background, abstract, claims, drawings, and charts. I even drew a picture of a baby wearing the monitoring device. Moreover, Devicix provided an "exploded" view of the baby monitoring system, detailing each piece, as well as circuit schematics.

Finally, on November 4, at 1:18 p.m., I filed the provisional with the United States Patent Office for a fee of $110. I passed the provisional patent and the receipt on to Halo Innovations and felt thankful to have the project off my plate temporarily. Wyatt and I were gearing up for a trip to Florida so he could meet Dad and Auntie Kim, and I needed a getaway. The project had started to cause stress and tension between Chad and me. I resented him for not helping me more, but he didn't know how to proceed anymore than I did.

I expected him to be more of a cheerleader. Mostly we just avoided each other—he hung out in the basement and I waited for a response from Halo.

For weeks, the provisional patent bounced back and forth between attorneys like a hot potato. Halo's attorneys worked to determine if a full patent could be secured on the product and if there would be freedom to operate—meaning we could sell it without infringing on someone else's patent and winding up in court. I'd extensively researched the landscape for similar patents and provided a detailed list to Halo's attorneys. The field was thick with lofty aspirations made by entrepreneurial types who'd never brought a product to the market: twenty-one patents for wearable garments with devices that monitored lack of movement and/or breathing; four patents for measuring oxygen levels; three patents for video systems for monitoring; thirteen patents for devices that could be installed under a crib or mattress to detect movement; and ten miscellaneous patents that ranged from a hood that went over the infant's head to detect exhaled breaths to electrodes applied to a baby's skin to monitor physiological conditions. The sheer volume of patents out there frightened me, but I truly believed we had significant differences that could lead to us securing our own patent. I appreciated the views of forward-thinking patent attorneys like Suneel, who argued that "the first one to market should win."

My stomach felt like it was wrapped around a lead grenade as I waited for the final word from Halo's attorneys. Then the bomb dropped into my Outlook Express Inbox on Tuesday, November 25. In a lengthy e-mail, Bill reported that his patent attorney's review of our provisional patent led him to believe that "1) There is a LOT of prior art on sensing systems; 2) Your patent application does not appear to infringe any current patents; 3) There are expired patents, however, that your claims would be similar too, thus 4) Your claims would probably not be allowed because of this prior art. They feel there is very little room for new IP in this category. That was disappointing to us and I'm sure it is to you."

With crushed spirits, I read on: "In the interest of full disclosure on my part, Amy, I must tell you that we filed a provisional patent, too, several weeks ago. It was based on my notarized inventor log from before our first meeting and a conversation I had with our manufacturer on a rollover concept in June. This communication occurred months before I was introduced to you. Our attorneys suggested we file a provisional just to make sure we covered the content of my notes. Again, these notes were made and witnessed before our meeting. I had been thinking of the concept for some time and it was truly ironic that you had, too." *He had filed before me.* I almost threw up. "I'm not sure our provisional has any more chance of patentability than yours, frankly. The field is just very crowded with prior art and the patent office is being much more difficult these days.

"This puts us both in a tough spot," Bill wrote. "We (Halo) need to make a business decision as to whether or not it is worth the expense of getting into this category without any IP protection. You probably need to ask yourself the same question. It is a difficult one, I know. If we decide *not* to enter this category, I would be happy to help you with your pursuit of the project. If we decide to pursue a monitor at Halo, I am not sure I can help you. I also am not sure if you can help us. Perhaps we could define a role for you in the marketing of the product in the long run, but that is really hard to say at this point."

I slammed my laptop shut. I couldn't help but be angry. I wondered why Bill hadn't mentioned his inventor log or the conversation with the manufacturer during our initial meeting in August. Or when I handed over my entire business plan chock full of marketing ideas, statistics, and projected revenue spreadsheets. Or how about when I sent him my provisional patent. I felt used and betrayed. I felt both of these helpless emotions—and more that I couldn't describe. Then, as if reading the e-mail the first time wasn't enough, I read it again later that afternoon.

By evening, my body and mind were numb. I felt so royally screwed over, and when I cried about it to Chad, he insisted, "We'll get it done."

"How?" I asked him, hoping he actually had the answer. "I don't know where to go from here."

"This is meant to be," he said matter-of-factly, and all I could do was stare at the washing machine, thinking, *You haven't done a thing to move this project forward. Don't you tell me it's meant to be.*

I called Suneel and relayed the situation to him. It was hard for him to say exactly where I stood from a legal standpoint because he was only semi-involved with the provisional patent. I couldn't afford to have him fully involved. I forwarded him the e-mail from Halo and his initial thought was that Bill was an honest guy, and I knew deep down inside he was, too. I was just so thoroughly disappointed.

"Maybe he didn't go about things the best way by not sharing his information sooner," said Suneel, "but he seems genuine."

"I know," I said. "I'm probably just taking it out on him because I want this to get done so badly."

Suneel reminded me about my notes and my inventor's log that went back almost seventeen months, right after Isabelle passed away, and that those documents would show that I had been working on the idea since then.

"Make sure you hang on to that," Suneel said. "You never know when you'll need it."

I hung up with Suneel and cried again. The last thing I wanted was any kind of legal wrangling. Instead, I half-hoped Halo *would* create the baby monitor themselves. Then it would be out there and I could stop thinking about it. I didn't really care about the money I'd miss out on or the recognition. That wasn't important to me. The question I was stuck with now, with another New Year looming only six short weeks away, was where would I take the project next year?

Wyatt and I spent a week in late November with my family in Florida, and the vacation was refreshing. In talking with Mom, I decided to let the news from Halo and my vision for the Izzy Bell percolate throughout December as I focused on the holidays and my growing little boy. But there was that little stopwatch spinning in the back of my mind reminding me that I only had six months to file a full patent or my provisional patent date stamp would be null and void. I needed help, again, and I didn't have the energy to look anymore. So I prayed and prayed and prayed some more that I would get an answer.

* * *

The gates of grief swung wide open each time I went to the support group, but there was something so healing about being with those parents. There were families who were years ahead of us in their journey, and, inevitably, each month there was a new person or couple who joined our group. I saw the same pain I felt in those first weeks and months reflected on their faces. And like clockwork, another new couple arrived at our December support group meeting. I liked, for the new couple's sake, that most of the session focused on parents' stories of what got them through those first awful months after their babies died. Surprisingly, one mom pointed to the *SIDS Survival Guide* as being her saving grace. One dad shared stories of his spouse's strength, and a mom mentioned the unwavering support of her family. Chad and I nodded in agreement. I didn't have to think very long before the Izzy Bell baby monitor came to my mind. I didn't share my thoughts, because no one in our group knew about my work on the project.

Then the new mom, calm in demeanor and almost ethereal, said, "I think we are given by God exactly what we need at any given moment to get us through. Maybe it's not something we'll have or need forever, but it's what gets us through."

A few parents straightened at the mention of God. We rarely talked about religion in the group, which consisted of mixed races and cultures. But for me, it wasn't the mention of God that sent my mind reeling. I sat in silence as a bleak picture formed in my mind. *What if the purpose of the Izzy Bell project was simply to get me through the hardest part of losing Isabelle? What if that was its sole purpose? Not formal patents or commercialization or eventual worldwide distribution? God, no, is it true? Did you give me that just to get me through?*

The thought crushed me and I slouched down in my chair, wedged between the hard plastic and the oblong table, and surrounded by a dozen other parents. I let my head fall into my hands and I cried. Chad rubbed my shoulder and I imagined no one thought anything of my near-silent whimpering. Tears ran rampant in that room and tissue boxes lined the tables.

I shared my horrific thought with Chad on the drive home. He listened, then asked, too calmly for my liking, "Well, what if it was just to get you through? It's gotten you this far, hasn't it?"

Even though it was twenty degrees and windy outside, my cheeks burned. I wished I'd never gone to the meeting or listened to that girl, who, by the way, seemed way too grounded for having just lost a child.

"You might be right, on some level," I said acidly. "But it's just not the same level I'm on. From here I can only see the time, energy, and hope I've poured into this project. The plans I've made for the future, the people I've shared this project with…"

I dropped my head into my hands again and Chad was quiet during the ride home. I thought about the path that had brought me to that moment. What were those overwhelmingly strong feelings? The ones that propelled me forward and assured me that the Izzy Bell project was what I was supposed to put my time into? Was I the one who was wrong in assuming the whole purpose was to bring the product to the market? Had I misread God's signs? I felt defeated. Deflated. Angry at God and angry at his methods.

The next day I called Mom. "Really? Could it really be that the Izzy Bell project was just to get me through?" I asked her.

"Maybe," Mom said, and that crushed me just as much as the original realization. I'd hoped that her response would be a resounding, *Heaven's no, Amy! You are on a mission from God and that mission is to bring this baby monitor to the market. Wipe your tears and go, go, go! You've got work to do.*

"I don't think I could ever accept it if that's the way this is supposed to turn out," I said.

"I know," Mom said. "I felt so angry at God in the hospital, but Kim kept telling me that we had to believe in him and accept his plan. That would be the only way we'd go to Heaven and see Isabelle again."

I was surprised at my little sister's insightfulness. She saw so much more than I realized and felt so much more than she let on.

"I feel tricked by God," I said after a short silence.

"God works in mysterious ways, I guess," Mom said. "Ways you and I will probably never understand."

We talked a little more and when I hung up, I sobbed. Again, again, again. It felt like I was losing Isabelle all over again. I curled up next to Wyatt on the floor and just watched him. He reached over and touched my face. In that moment, my heart sang and the conflicting emotions subsided a little. If I was going to do this, be a true follower of God, I had to do it all the time. Especially now. I thought again about dot-to-dot puzzles and how I'd been so convinced six months before that this baby monitor was my destiny, my new purpose. What I didn't realize on that day, though, when all of my stars seemed to align and my dots seemed to connect, was that there were—throughout history—puzzles that were never meant to be finished for one reason or another.

I rolled Wyatt over. "Tummy time, buddy," I said. "Your sister loved tummy time. Let me tell you all about her."

Chapter Twenty-One

On Christmas Eve, I was sick with stomach pains and a fever of 101 degrees that wouldn't drop. Chad had to work and I sent Wyatt to Andre's house to hopefully prevent him from catching my illness. I lay on the leather couch in our living room and stared at the ceiling. There was something so special about our house. Even when the three levels were empty of visitors, the structure bustled with fullness, alive with a comfortable energy. On that day, though, the house felt painfully vacant—so incredibly void of life that I swore I heard the lonesome structure weeping. Or maybe it was the winter sleet shower outside. Either way, we were alone. The house and me.

With my body hunched forward and my right hand cradling my stomach, I wearily climbed the stairs toward our bedroom and the comfort of our king-size bed. With each step, the house let out a croak of despair, and, like a rehearsed duo, I matched each note with a moan of my own. At the top of the stairs, I bypassed our bedroom and headed straight to Wyatt's room…Isabelle's room. I didn't even know what to call the room anymore. Isabelle's name still decorated the wall above the crib, along with Wyatt's name below, and a few pink accents helped to keep her memory alive without making the room appear too girly.

I shuffled across the wooden floor to the dresser and touched the small, silver jewelry box with Isabelle's name and baptism date engraved on the front. Inside I found the white plastic rings that were fastened around her newborn ankles the day we brought her home. I sniffed the plastic pieces and I smelled nothingness. Synthetic, man-made materials. Emptiness. Sadness. Definitely not the smell of Isabelle. These items of hers, they were just things. They couldn't coo or swat at my earrings or fall asleep on my chest. They couldn't even smell like her, and that's what I needed, to be reminded of her smell. I gasped, horrified that I couldn't remember her scent. It had only been a year-and-a-half. Too soon to let even the tiniest detail slip away. The hot flash of fear sent me on a rampage throughout the house that—in the end—would be life changing.

The house's walls trembled with each of my sobs, and when I pushed open the pocket door to the upstairs closet where we kept a trio of pink bins that stored the evidence of Isabelle's four months of existence, the house seemed to bellow with me. Clothes. Toys. Baby bottles. No. 2 unused diapers. I pulled out a pink and white quilted baby blanket with the words "Some Bunny Loves You" on the front and a picture of a floppy-eared rabbit on the back. I held the blanket close to me, smelled it, but, again, no smell.

I turned quickly and moved into my office just down the hall, the door screeching before it hit the wall with a thud. I scooped up the three pictures of Isabelle I kept on my desk and carried them with the blanket to our bedroom.

"Please God," I whispered, pressing my eyes closed. "Please let me hold my baby again."

I reasoned that if I could just hold her one more time, rub my lips across her forehead, and take in her baby scent, I would commit that feeling and her smell to memory, maintain it somehow. I would never be so careless as to let my mind forget again.

I opened my eyes, but nothing happened. So I rushed to my closet, searched the top shelf with my fingertips, and pulled down the pair of ratty jeans I'd worn in the hospital. Then I found the black and white tank top and put that on, too. Chill bumps stood at attention on my arms. The house began to sway and the walls seemed to step forward, closing in around me. I melted like Silly Putty into a fetal position, then crawled into bed with my pictures and the blanket and I sobbed. I sobbed because I missed her. I sobbed because she would miss so much. I sobbed because her life was too short and the rest of my life was way too long.

Only the house knows when I fell asleep, but I awoke with a start an hour later. The walls of the house had realigned themselves and stood tall once again. The room was quiet and the pains in my stomach were gone. I touched my forehead and it was sweaty, but it wasn't hot anymore. I slid out of the tall bed, leaving the pictures and the blanket tucked safely next to my pillow. Downstairs I found the energy to sweep the kitchen floor, and it was during that simple act of sweeping that the stack of holiday greeting cards on the counter caught my attention. Surreally, the room darkened, a projector kicked on inside my head, and my memory played the dream I'd had while sleeping.

It was Christmas Eve and we celebrated at my father-in-law's heavily decorated rambler just down the street from our home. A white, cotton clothesline ran from the kitchen, through the dining room and into the living room where it was clipped to an eye hook just above the front door. All sizes of wrapped presents encircled with ribbons and brightly colored bows were fastened with wooden clips to the clothesline. Adults were laughing and children were running around, and one by one the gifts were unclipped from the clothesline and dispersed.

After all of the presents were opened and the "oohs" and "ahhs" subsided, I leaned over Chad's shoulder and whispered, "I didn't get a present."

Chad turned to me, his forehead wrinkled, then looked at the empty clothesline. "Hmmm. That's strange."

Wyatt was on Chad's shoulders and he pointed to the far wall in the kitchen. "There!" he shouted excitedly. "Mommy, you forgot one!"

I whirled around and zeroed in on a small, ivory-colored envelope clipped to the very top of the clothesline, half hidden by the cupboard. "Amy" was written on the front in a chicken-scratch print. With all eyes on me, I unclipped the card. I was embarrassed that Chad's family had witnessed my uneasiness over not receiving a gift, yet I was thankful I was not completely forgotten.

I tore open the envelope. The cover of the card was simple with a traditional wintertime scene reproduced on the same ivory paper as the envelope. A small, snow-covered house had smoke billowing from its chimney like puffs of happiness. Evergreen trees protectively encircled the perimeter. Outdoor lights illuminated a cobblestone path as a horse-drawn carriage rolled by. I opened the card and handwritten in black ink were the words, "Write that book. Love God and Isabelle."

Yes. I had a book to write.

* * *

I made time to write in my journal every day and it helped me to loosen my grasp on the Izzy Bell project. And again, like the winter before, my thoughts turned to volunteering. A few days after Christmas I had lunch with my friend Jen, who was my most-trusted sounding board next to my mother. As if keyed to the same song, we curled up across the table from each other at a coffee shop and poured out our hearts about becoming more involved in doing something good. Something to positively change peoples' lives. The week before we'd attended an informational event organized by a nonprofit group called Breaking Free that served women and girls involved in systems of abuse, exploitation, and prostitution/sex-trafficking. It was Jen's idea to attend and I gladly agreed. There was something brewing in each of us, and that two hours set off flares in our psyches, illuminating all of the causes out there and all of the people who could use our help.

Jen lived in south Minneapolis and she carried McDonald's coupons in her purse that she gave out to panhandlers rather than cash. When the weather turned colder, she stuffed the back of her car full of blankets and offered them to homeless people. I organized an event in Isabelle's memory on the Saturday after Christmas at Feed My Starving Children, a group "committed to feeding God's starving children hungry in body and spirit." As a group of fourteen, we weighed, bagged, and boxed nutritional pouches consisting of rice, extruded soy nuggets, dehydrated vegetables, vitamins, minerals, and a vegetarian chicken flavoring.

Volunteering nourished my wounded spirit, so I continued. I collected items for a baby supply drive at Cross of Peace church. I donated toys and clothes to the Southern Valley Alliance for Battered Women. I bought material, sewing needles, and thread, bundled them together and gave them to an organization that taught women in India how to sew, make clothes for themselves, and make clothes to sell. I wanted to do more, give more, but there was a proverbial dark cloud hanging over me, reminding me that I was no closer to finding an investor or partner for the Izzy Bell project. And how could I start another project when I hadn't finished the most important one? Sure, I had relinquished control somewhat, but that didn't take away the feeling that I wasn't keeping up my end of the bargain for Isabelle.

Equally disturbing were the columns and columns of home foreclosure notices that inked up the legal section of the local newspaper. A news anchor gave a doomsday report right before President Obama was elected into office and he called our economic struggle "The Great Recession."

I hadn't heard from Devicix after the e-mails I'd sent before the holidays inquiring about a partnership. I assumed they struggled like everyone else and weren't particularly interested in investing in a not-for-sure venture during our current "economic landslide."

I grasped at straws in hopes of puffing a little life back into the Izzy Bell project, but each time I came up short. Suneel recommended I pitch the Izzy Bell concept to another medical device engineering firm called Dymedix.

"What have you got to lose?" he asked encouragingly, offering far more support than was required by our agreement. Again, I listened and sent a brief e-mail introducing myself to the director of technology, then cut straight to the point. "I currently have a provisional patent filed and am hoping to bring this product to the retail market; however, I am in need of assistance/partnership. Is this something you'd be interested in learning more about?"

Reinhold Henke responded within a few days and we scheduled a meeting for later that month. We had trouble coordinating schedules with his team members and the meeting was pushed back to January 27. But at 4 a.m. that day, I woke to Raven howling in the doorway of Wyatt's room where I slept on a full-size bed next to his bassinet. There was a loud beeping and I rolled out of bed wearily to wake Chad.

"Is that our carbon monoxide detector?" I asked, shoving his shoulder.

Chad sprang out of bed like I'd slapped him and ran to the device he'd installed in our hallway only six months earlier.

"It says move to fresh air!" he shouted, and I rushed into the nursery. It was one of the first times since his birth that our restless sleeper had slumbered a solid eight hours without waking.

"I think we have carbon monoxide poisoning!" I hollered, grabbing Raven by the collar and waking Wyatt, who looked at me suspiciously out of sleepy eyes. I wrapped him in a thick blanket and we stood in the open doorway, frigid January air spilling into our toxic home. Several police cars and an ambulance arrived within minutes. Initial readings were taken and we were quickly shuttled into the lit-up interior of an ambulance waiting by the curb. Chad and I received visual once-overs and were cleared, but a pulse oximeter was placed on Wyatt's big toe to measure his oxygen levels.

I looked at Chad, whose saddened eyes mirrored the ache in my chest. Isabelle was outfitted with a pulse oximeter on her big toe during her stay at Children's Hospital. I closed my eyes and before the tears could spill over, a squeal of delight pulled me from my sad memory. Wyatt poked and pulled at the funny clip that turned his big toe red with its infrared light. I laughed, too, and when the screen blinked a large "100," I exhaled hard.

"He's absolutely fine," the lady paramedic said and let Wyatt play a little longer with the clip.

Discharged from the ambulance, we were instructed to steer clear of our house until it was aired out and a new furnace was installed. With an officer's consent, I scurried inside, packed two duffel bags and joined Chad to load up Wyatt, the dog, and two cats into Chad's truck. We drove one block to Chad's dad's house, where we set up camp in his basement. By then it was 6 a.m., and Chad had to get ready for work.

Unfortunately I had to cancel my meeting with Dymedix so I could meet contractors at the house for estimates on a new furnace. Frustrated, I sent a message to Reinhold Henke and asked if I could e-mail him my business plan for review instead. From there we could determine if the project was a good fit for his company.

After thirteen e-mails over the course of five weeks and $6,000 for a new furnace, I received a response in early February from Reinhold Henke regarding the project. After a "fair amount of time" reviewing and discussing the product and business plan, Dymedix didn't foresee involvement in any new ventures for the next couple of years. You know, the economy and all. Moreover, Reinhold wrote, "At this time, Dymedix is not structured to take on the additional risks involved with entering the consumer market and taking on the added liability stemming from offering a medical type product for public use."

Reinhold and his team members took a look, though, and that was all I'd asked… Unfortunately, it wasn't all I'd hoped for. They'd been intrigued by the prospect and I couldn't fault them for being cautious. I thanked Reinhold earnestly and exhaled the last bit of energy I had for the Izzy Bell project.

* * *

The buzz around town, according to the local business publications, was that most investors felt the same way as Dymedix: gridlocked and overtly cautious. And with the negative news of the economy infiltrating daily life right down to dinner table discussions, I found myself embracing the financial downturn. Selfishly, the country's money woes gave me an out. It felt acceptable now to tell my friends and family members when they asked what was new with the Izzy Bell project that I still pursued it, "but with the economy and all…" The E-word sent their heads nodding and I imagined their minds reeled with snapshots of their own dire financial footing: plummeting stocks, rising costs of essentials, potential job loss, and, worse, the probability of being one paycheck away from financial ruin.

So with the economy belly-flopping onto everyone's center stage, the waves of its encumbrance took the focus off of me and offered me a life raft with which to float to shore. Deflated, I tucked the Izzy Bell project away, just for the winter, I told myself. I'd known from the first meeting with Devicix more than a year-and-a-half before that I was the little fish in the big pond—the perch trying to keep up with the northern—but I'd hoped, no, *prayed,* that one of those big fish would take me under his fin. I hoped the patents and manufacturing reps and product implementation charts would find a way of working themselves out. I wasn't thoroughly washed up, but I was done for now—to save my sanity and to save my marriage. The prototype and two-drawer file full of research documents I'd collected over the year-and-a-half sat safely in my office closet, easily accessible should an interested party step forward. But the papers didn't clutter my kitchen table anymore, and they didn't consume my every thought.

* * *

At the beginning of March, Chad spent several days and more than $100 outfitting my laptop and his mom's computer with cameras and microphones. We were taking a nine-day trip to Playa del Secreto, a small, ocean-side community half an hour south of Cancun, but were having serious anxiety about leaving Wyatt. Our friends Joe and Leslie had rented a twelve-bedroom house on the ocean, Villa Sol y Luna, for their wedding and had invited their closest friends for the occasion.

"I'm not going," I told Chad the night before as I held Wyatt in my arms. He was nine months old and I'd spent every day with him since his birth. Nine days would be the end of me.

"But we already paid for our plane tickets," Chad said.

I shook my head. "I don't care about the money. I'm not going."

Somehow Chad talked me into dropping Wyatt off the next morning at his mom's house, and seeing my son's excitement for

Grandma and Grandpa put me at ease. The flight was smooth, I read the whole way, and the house in Mexico was a castle fit for royalty. Each couple had their own luxurious room, and I felt like a princess with all of the time in the world to read, write, swim, and succumb to the sun. Relaxation never tasted so sweet. We fed the resident alligator raw chicken, played volleyball in the pool, and received massages on the rooftop deck. The ambiance made being away from Wyatt a little easier, and thankfully our Skype connection worked perfectly so we were able to check in on him daily.

Part of me struggled to enjoy myself too much. I felt guilty when I laughed too hard or went more than a few hours without openly missing Isabelle. I struggled with finding a balance that would allow me to properly maintain her memory.

Sunday, March 8

I was overwhelmed with grief for Isabelle this evening. I walked along the beach as the sun was setting and I felt so close to Heaven, to Isabelle, that I heard myself whisper, "I can feel you." I begged God to let me see her one more time, to let me hold her little hand, or even to look back and see my footprints in the sand next to tiny baby steps. It was a stretch, I knew, and although I never got a physical sign of Isabelle, I could feel her. I could feel the warmth I felt when I had held her here on earth.

I walked along the beach for nearly an hour, dodging waves, picking seashells, and marveling—as so many people do near the ocean—at the beauty God has created. It's very possible that the ocean, the sand and the waves, are there not simply as water bordering land, but as a taste of what Heaven will be like.

There wasn't a fluent Spanish speaker in our bunch, which made our outings to Puerto Morelos for shopping and to Playa del Carmen for dinner bumbling experiences in foreign travel. Chad and I were in a shop when he found a shelf full of rocks with names painted on each one and the Mayan meaning of the name printed on the back. He searched for Isabelle's name, but never found it. Just as we were about to walk away, he plucked a rock off the shelf.

"Wyatt!" he said excitedly. He flipped the rock over and read the meaning: "Invincible."

My breath caught as Chad closed his eyes and squeezed the rock. "God I hope so," he whispered.

The day before we left to come home, a group of us went to Selvatica, where we swung through the jungle via zip lines and jumped off cliffs into a cenote—one of many sacred and secluded pools of crystal blue water in the Riviera Maya. Standing on a metal stairway tucked 150 feet above the ground in the tops of trees, Chad turned to look at me.

"I never thought I'd see you swinging through a Mexican jungle!" he laughed.

I smiled and kissed him. My world had cracked wide open. I was so far out of my comfort zone that I ironically felt more comfortable than ever before. For the first time in my life, I didn't feel like the scared girl in the corner refusing to climb the stairs or get on the ride, fixated on the horror that would undoubtedly find me. No, on this particular day in a Mexican jungle, I was second in line behind my husband. I took the stairs two at a time, my harness pulled tight around me, my helmet secured, and my fear slapped away by the gentle beating of angels' wings.

* * *

As winter's chill gave way to warmer weather, my life started to seem, dare I say it, normal. Chad often had to ask "why?" on the days I seemed overly sad or distracted. We were back to being frustrated by work, family, or unpaid bills. Life had lost its sharp edge and it felt safe again to feel frustrated by work, family, or unpaid bills. Chad still managed a Walgreens store and I'd agreed to a full-time position with the newspaper as associate publisher. Everyone knew me there. They knew my story. It was easy, safe, and comfortable. I didn't think it was a long-term gig for me, but it fit for the time being. Truthfully, I wanted to be writing again.

"It's a transitional position," Janelle said one night when she was in town from Texas. "Think of it as a stepping stone to greater things."

"I am pretty awesome," I said, sipping the remainder of my wine. "I'll do something spectacular someday."

Janelle's giant blue eyes smiled at me. "You've already created two someones that are especially spectacular. Isabelle and Wyatt."

Once upon a time, the title of associate publisher would have thrilled me to my core. I was honored that the employees spoke so highly of me that the owner offered me the position, but I really did not care about the job like I wanted to care about the place where I would spend forty hours per week. I was more concerned with our new conundrum of putting Wyatt into day care. I was determined, if I worked full time, to arrange a schedule in such a way that I felt like Wyatt got all of me when we were together. I didn't want to be an "in-a-minute mom."

Chad and I tentatively discussed day care options, both remarking on several occasions that we couldn't believe we even considered the prospect of putting him in day care. I could admit without much guilt that I wasn't a stay-at-home mom, and Chad agreed that he wasn't a stay-at-home dad. And a gentle conversation with Wyatt's pediatrician the next week confirmed that it was probably time to think about day care anyway.

"So what do you have planned for Wyatt in terms of social interaction?" Dr. Gears asked. There were oodles of colorful Disney character pins dangling from her lanyard and Wyatt swatted at them.

"What do you mean? Playing with Mommy isn't enough?" I joked, prying his tiny fingers from her name badge.

"One-year-olds are very curious and like to play with other kids. It's also important for Wyatt to learn at this age that he will not always be the center of attention," she said. "And it's important for him to share—toys and time."

Hoping for an "a-ha! moment" that would land us at the perfect day care, I called numerous centers and in-home providers, and simultaneously prayed for God to guide me. Time after time I thought about Carla. More than once I pushed the thought aside, made more calls, and visited two in-home day cares close to our house, as well as a child care center only steps away from the newspaper office. I wasn't convinced that any of them were right for Wyatt.

And then the dreams came.

They weren't vividly clear dreams. My dreams typically possessed a murky undertone that offered only foggy recollections when I woke. But these were definitely dreams about Carla, her house, and the outdoor toys that had playfully littered her front yard on the afternoons I'd picked up Isabelle.

When I confessed my dreams to Chad, I was surprised to learn that he had thought about Carla, too. I was at odds with the situation and with the mixed bag of feelings I'd lugged around for the past two years. I'd held tightly to the conclusion that Carla was somehow responsible for Isabelle's death, though I didn't anymore.

Yet it seemed that God and Isabelle were trying to tell me something.

Chapter Twenty-Two

Moving on our instincts, Chad left Carla a voicemail message. He wanted to gauge her interest in caring for Wyatt and, finally, after two days she called him back.

"She wants to meet with us," Chad said. "She said that her first reaction was definitely against watching Wyatt, but she took a couple of days and decided that if we were okay with her caring for our child, she'd be okay, too."

I pushed Wyatt's pudgy feet into his Nikes. "At least she was honest," I said. Over the two days of waiting for her to respond, I'd concluded that this decision had to be left completely up to Isabelle and God. I wanted no part of it. I asked God for a definite feeling when I walked into Carla's house again and an instant reaction from Wyatt when he saw Carla. But I had no feeling when I walked into Carla's house—good, bad, or indifferent. The birds still sang outside and the breeze still blew through her open windows. The world didn't stop and Wyatt kept breathing as I held him in my arms. Carla was visibly nervous and I didn't blame her. I was nervous, too. She greeted us and we went downstairs to the area she reserved specifically for the day care children. The half-moon–shaped table was still there, the toys were arranged in the same colorful bins and totes, and there was still a separate room for sleeping infants and toddlers.

Is that the room Isabelle was in? I wondered, realizing I didn't know for sure whether Isabelle had taken naps in the room on the main floor or in this lower level room. I peered in, waiting for some horrific flashes of Isabelle's last moments to engulf me, but the room was still. We sat in a circle on the floor, and Wyatt leaped out of my arms. He smiled openly and lunged for a truck.

199

"Broom, broom," he gurgled as he pushed the truck along the floor.

"Do you like that truck?" Carla asked him and he put the front tire in his mouth.

Carla looked at us. "I'm really honored that you called me," she said, her eyes watery.

I looked to Chad, who clearly wasn't going to say anything. He was too busy reveling in Wyatt's apparent happiness. "I thought a lot about it and called several other day cares...and I prayed about it," I said hesitantly, still not sure how people would react to me throwing God into everyday conversations. I looked up and Carla was nodding. "I also had a dream that he went to day care here."

Carla told us that her six-year-old daughter, Wendy, still talked about Isabelle. "Sometimes out of nowhere she'll say, 'Isabelle's okay and she's in Heaven, right, Mom?'"

My heart lurched and I swallowed hard, and it was Chad's turn to get teary. I looked around the room and tried to feel angry at this woman, but mostly I felt like Isabelle was right there with me, urging me to look around and feel whatever I needed to feel, and then to move on. To forgive.

We told Carla we'd go home and talk about it, and as we pulled out of her driveway I assessed my feelings. My emotions definitely weren't overwhelming like I'd asked God to make them. Surprisingly, the strongest feeling I had was that Wyatt should go to Carla's for day care. Not that he *had* to go, but that he could go and that he would be okay.

* * *

April brought with it the usual rainy days, but also those first glorious moments of spring. I drank in the sweetest Friday evening like it was pink lemonade with the perfect blend of sugar and tart. I delighted in the smell of raw earth, freshly mowed lawns, and periodic whiffs of fires from neighbors' yards, burning off the remnants of fall and winter. I relaxed on the bench in Isabelle's Garden, thinking that spring offered a fresh start for me more so than the New Year. I felt Isabelle's presence around me often, encircling me with a comfort that can rarely be found in the real world, but must come, I thought, from the afterworld. I did my best to let God guide me. I was learning and I figured the process of spirituality was different for everyone. So I did what felt right in my heart. I talked openly with God. I told him about my day. I shared the multitude of areas in which I struggled with decisions and did my best to listen, more often than not perplexed by what exactly it was that I was listening for.

After the Feed My Starving Children event in December, and our miscellaneous acts of charity, Jen and I started a volunteer group that gathered on two occasions to make sandwiches for homeless people in Minneapolis. We were up to twenty-three members on our Facebook page, and in starting the group Jen and I had whimsical musings that we could bring some relief to the Minneapolis homeless crisis. Little did we know that a mere year later, we would be selected to serve on the steering committee of a Minneapolis effort called Downtown Congregations to End Homelessness. And a mere six months after that, Jen and I would work side by side as lead coordinators for a new fifty-bed emergency homeless shelter. And it was during those nights when we sweated in the hot kitchen to create meals for our homeless friends that I felt closest to God.

* * *

Mom and Kim came from Florida the first week in June, and we scurried around like ants on a disturbed hill to pack as much togetherness into one week as possible. They bought assorted annuals, hydrangeas, and two climbing clematis for Isabelle's Garden, and on a beautiful Thursday evening Chad's family joined us as we planted a white-blossoming crabapple tree in Isabelle's memory. Chad dug the wide hole while I offered pencils and paper to anyone who wanted to write a note to Isabelle to place in the ground, offering strength and nourishment to the rooting tree. I watched as family members found quiet spots in our large yard and peered into the distance, much as they'd done more than a year before during her birthday balloon release, imagining what message to pass on to the little girl who'd been with us such a short time. My sister made pins with small dragonfly appliqués and my niece, Lexy, passed them out as I read a dragonfly story I'd found on the Internet by Walter Dudley Cavert:

"In the bottom of an old pond lived some grubs who could not understand why none of their group ever came back after crawling up the lily stems to the top of the water. They promised each other that the next one who was called to make the upward climb would return and tell what had happened to him.

"Soon one of them felt an urgent impulse to seek the surface; he rested himself on the top of a lily pad and went through a glorious transformation which made him a dragonfly with beautiful wings. In vain he tried to keep his promise. Flying back and forth over the pond, he peered down at his friends below. Then he realized that even if they could see him they would not recognize such a radiant creature as one of their own.

"The fact that we cannot see our friends or communicate with them after the transformation which we call death is no proof that they cease to exist."

Two days later we celebrated Wyatt's first birthday. He was clearly overwhelmed by the people, the noise, and the activity, but he was a good sport, considering all of the people, the noise, and the activity. He even showed the crowd he was "So big!" by taking his first steps alone. I was inspired when I watched Wyatt learning to walk. Step, step, fall. Step, step, fall. I recognized frustration on his little wrinkled forehead and in the purse of his lips, but mostly I saw determination in his big, brown eyes. And when his tiny hands clutched multiple toys, only to have them tumble to the floor with another misstep, he watched them scatter, then pushed to his feet again, bypassing his knees all together. When exhaustion finally did set in, he plopped down with a toy in hand, his work done for the day. I guessed that the next day he would walk just as far and collect just as many toys, because he'd proven to himself that he was capable. Or maybe he'd go just a little bit farther.

* * *

That summer, I recognized that July would always be an especially difficult month for me. I would recall the Fourth of July when we dressed Isabelle in a cute denim skirt, white polo shirt, and tiny white socks with red, white, and blue dangling beads. Just as quickly, I would be faced with the reality that the end of the month brought her Heaven Day. I expected that I would always navigate the end of July warily, steering clear of the library, flinching painfully at ambulances, and wondering if I shouldn't take the last Monday of the month off of work, just to be safe. It was my reality now. I felt it, I lived it, and, somehow, I got through it.

I felt especially close and especially far from Isabelle on the Monday before her Heaven Day. I was running late for work and was halfway out of the driveway when I realized I'd forgotten my cell phone. I rushed back into the house, only to be stopped in my tracks by the brightest blue butterfly I'd ever seen, almost iridescent, lounging on the wall in my dining room. I stepped closer to admire its wings, trimmed in white, and the orangeish-yellow spots on its lower wings. I laughed a bit hysterically, surprised by its size, and walked toward the butterfly. It swooped and dove around my head, then made its way to the kitchen where it landed on my favorite sunflower picture—a cheap Van Gogh reproduction.

"That's not a real flower!" I laughed giddily, and the butterfly danced around me again, landing on the door that opened to the backyard.

I gently approached, opened the screen door, and the butterfly flew outside, only to swoop back in front of my face again before flying out of sight. I walked outside, but the butterfly was gone. I sat on the deck with my eyes closed, feeling the morning sun on my face.

"Thank you," I whispered.

I sat awhile longer, then went back inside, collected my cell phone, and arrived at the newspaper office with a cushion of comfort beneath me. Once at my desk, I pulled up the Internet and did a Google search: blue butterfly Minnesota. There were countless search results for the Karner blue butterfly. I clicked on the Minnesota Department of Natural Resources link and saw a picture of the exact butterfly that had been in my dining room. I read out loud: "The Karner blue butterfly is a federally endangered species and is only found in one location in Minnesota. This small, beautiful butterfly inhabits oak savanna and requires lupine plants on which to lay its eggs. Oak savannas are one of the rarest native plant communities in Minnesota." I bit my lower lip. I had no idea if oak savannah trees existed in our area or what a lupine plant even looked like. I considered conducting more research, but decided I didn't need to read any more to know what I already knew deep in my heart. Isabelle was okay. She was safe and she was okay.

I thought about the butterfly that had landed on my ankle after Isabelle's funeral and the beautiful blue creature inside my home that day, and I couldn't have known then that, in years to come, butterflies would make themselves a significant symbol in my life. They'd flitter by in the most unlikely of places, encircling my body at a park to the delighted screams of Wyatt and landing on my arm at the precise second I whispered my daughter's name.

I remembered a devotional I'd read that said God routinely gave us gifts throughout the day. We only had to be open enough to recognize them.

* * *

Isabelle's Heaven Day fell on a Sunday. Janelle had given me the books *The Christmas Box* and *The Christmas Box Miracle* by Richard Paul Evans that winter. In the first book, there was an angel statue at a cemetery and a mother who mourned the loss of her child at the base of the statue. The book had become a bestseller and more than eighty similar statues were erected throughout the country. So, for Isabelle's Heaven Day, I asked family members, as well as Jen and Marti, to join us at the *Christmas Box* Angel Statue at the nearby Maple Grove Arboretum.

July 26 was a beautiful day. Hot and sunny and full of life. We walked a short distance through the park along a path and found the statue up on a small hill, with perfectly manicured grass surrounding it. A pavilion was nearby. The base of the statue stood about five feet tall. The angel added another four feet in height, with an impressive wingspan. We took turns reading the words on the back of the statue and the precious quotes on the benches nearby. Jen and Marti had purchased a brick that would be inscribed and placed at the base of the statue in Isabelle's memory. There were already dozens of the bricks with engraved names and inscriptions, and plenty of room for more. It bothered me that someday—probably not too far from that day—all of the bricks would be inscribed with children's names.

I'd picked a variety of flowers from Isabelle's Garden at home and tied the stems together with raffia. I placed the flowers at the base of the angel's feet, next to a fresh white rose and other, dried-up flowers. Just as the tears welled on my lower lids, Wyatt began an impressive Spiderman-like scaling of my legs and proceeded to climb all over the angel statue. I peeled him off, thinking it seemed disrespectful to let him run rampant in such a sacred space. He lurched from my arms, ran in circles, and stomped on the bricks like he was squashing bugs. When he tired of stomping, he picked up a handful of sticks, threw them at the angel, and yelled, "Dah!" as a shower of sticks fell all around us.

"It's probably time to go," Chad whispered.

I nodded and scooped up our terrific little distraction.

* * *

The following year, with two-year-old Wyatt leading the way, we went back to the angel statue and decided to make the visit an annual tradition. This time we brought hot dogs and hamburgers to grill, and had a potluck under the pavilion with family and friends.

In the late afternoon, we took Wyatt fishing. It was the end of July, and he'd already lost two fishing poles in the lake. I suited him up in a life jacket and sat with him at the end of the dock while Chad worked on our pontoon boat. Wyatt didn't know how to cast, he didn't know how to sit still, and he didn't know how to reel in a fish. For everyone's safety, I'd taken the hook off the end of his line and tied a plastic worm there instead. I kept an eye on him as I paged through my *O, The Oprah Magazine*. Despite his excited yelling and stomping on the dock, being by the water was relaxing for me. I thought about my teenage years growing up on the lake, when I fished with Grandpa, and how those days remained such clear sepia-colored memories that turned out to be about so much more than fishing.

Grandpa was a solid, silly man who talked about God as if he were a classmate from high school. He sprinkled in comments about Jesus right after knock-knock jokes and just before he'd playfully threaten to put San Diego snails in my shoes. He called God "a keeper," which made total sense to me, since much of Grandpa's vocabulary centered on fishermen's lingo. I'd caught my first keeper, which came in the form of a plump sunfish, off the end of my parent's dock when Grandpa and Grandma made a special end-of-summer trip to our Minnesota home. Dropping a line with Grandpa on a Sunday morning wasn't the first thing on my teenager to-do list, but it sure beat going to church.

"You're never gonna catch a sunny with that much corn," I told Grandpa as he loaded up a king-size hook with niblets.

"Watch and learn, cupcake. I've done this a hundred times." He let the baited hook swing free as he adjusted the bobber, depressed the release, and sent the line whizzing through the air with a final plop in the lake.

"Right in the sun spot," he said triumphantly, speaking of that glimmering patch where the sun reflected off the water with blinding brightness. *Reel twice. Jerk. Reel twice. Jerk.* It was his method and he swore by it.

I shifted my pole from my left hand to my right and eyed the baitless hook at the end of my rod. I reluctantly pressed the release button and no sooner had the bobber hit the water and righted itself than it sank under the surface again.

"What the—" I jerked my pole spastically and pushed to my feet. Grandpa set down his rod and rushed to my side.

"Gently, gently," he whispered. "You don't want to lose him."

I stepped back, gave a final turn of the reel, and pulled up the fattest sunfish I'd ever seen, spinning and flailing and just barely hooked by a sliver of its lip.

"Looks like he got your corn." He reached for the line as I pulled the fish over the dock.

"I didn't use corn," I said, then steadied the fish in front of me and ever so carefully slipped my hand from front to back over its prickly fins, just the way Grandpa had taught me. "I had an empty hook."

"Hmmm. He must have seen something he liked," Grandpa reasoned, then looked out to his red and white bobber still resting atop the water.

Just as I freed the hook, the sunfish jerked in my hand, his top fin jutting into the soft flesh between my thumb and forefinger. He flipped out of my palm, bounced once on the dock, and flopped into the water. Grandpa and I each took a step forward to peer over the edge.

"And another one gets away," Grandpa said, reeled in his line, then cast to the same spot in the sun. "He was a keeper, too. Sure is funny how life works."

"What do you mean?" I asked, kneeling on the dock and stretching over the edge to rinse my hands in the water.

Grandpa slipped his rod into the dock pole again. "You'll learn, cupcake. You look the other way for one, maybe two seconds, and—" he clapped his hands together "—Kabam! Out of nowhere. Everything you think you know…well, it just changes."

I wasn't sure whether "Kabam!" was catching the fish or losing it, and I didn't ask Grandpa to clarify. Even at fourteen, I guessed he was talking about more than a sunfish. Somewhere in there I figured he was talking about God again.

I picked weeds off of Wyatt's line and he clapped his hands before taking the rod back from me. I flipped to the last page of the magazine, to Oprah's column called, "What I Know for Sure." The first time I saw the title, I thought it was pretty audacious of even Oprah to claim that she knew anything *for sure*. But that day, watching Wyatt pull up more weeds and call them fish, I thought Oprah was brilliant. Each month I read with curiosity the mystery of life Oprah had figured out, maybe not for the world at large, but at least for herself.

It got me thinking about the events of recent years and I wondered what it was that I could claim, at the age of thirty-four, I knew for sure. Well, it was safe to say that I knew for sure that losing a child wasn't the end of the world. It should be, but unfortunately time has no emotional ties and it keeps right on ticking. *Time did help me heal, but it was so much more than time alone,* I thought as I stroked Wyatt's fine blonde hair and hugged him around his life jacket. I never would have believed it, but that day on the dock I knew for sure that time and Wyatt's presence had dulled the ache of losing Isabelle. I guess I'd come to an agreement of sorts with grief. It would never leave me completely and, in some ways, I didn't want it gone. I wanted to keep that link to Isabelle. The pain proved that she was here, that I held her. That she had lived.

I knew for sure that I forever would have to allow myself those moments when my heart ached so badly it took my breath away. I knew that each time I would eventually move through the pain, that the aching would subside, but it would come again when I least expected it. A scab had formed, but it could break open so easily. The wound of loss would never completely heal, and I would carry my grief forever. Now, though, I had God to help me tote the load until I went home for good. Home with Isabelle.

I unwound Wyatt's fishing line from the dock pole and thought about my dearest friends, my mom and my sister, and Chad's family. I knew for sure that the truest tests of friendship came along during the hardest of times, and whoever delivered the adage, "Friends were made for a reason, a season, or a lifetime," well, that person knew something for sure.

God did have a plan for me. Maybe it didn't always coincide with the one I made for myself, but he was patient. It wasn't a coincidence that I'd lost Isabelle and found him. In my darkest hour, with no bait on my rusty hook, and no energy to cast a line, God still wanted me—when I was certain I didn't want him. He still came to me.

Kabam! Out of nowhere.

And now nothing will ever be the same.